Beyond the Last Oak

77 Ultra-short Stories of Mindfulness & Contemplation

James C. Washburn

Beyond the Last Oak

Copyright © 2017 by James C. Washburn

**Kal-Ba Publishing a division of
Cactus Moon Publications, LLC:**
Info@cactusmoonpublishing.com;
http://www.cactusmoonpublishing.com

Book cover photo: Mark Hirsch

ISBN: 978-0-9996965-0-7

For:

Tunisijuq Una

Guviagijaujuq

Takujuq Iluani

Tana Pisuttuq Saniani

Pinga Iji Mumiqtuq

Cover Photo

Permission for use of the cover photo granted by Mark Hirsch. Mark is a nationally recognized photographer, artist and inspiring speaker. He has spent twenty years as a photojournalist and editor. Clients include Getty Images, *The New York Times*, John Deer Corporation, and others.

Mark's book, *That Tree*, has been featured worldwide by organizations including but not limited to: CBS Sunday Morning, National Public Radio, *The Huffington Post*, NBC News, *The Daily Mail* (UK), *The Guardian*, The Sierra Club, *Denver Post*, *San Francisco Chronicle*, and *Chicago Tribune*.

That Tree is a beautiful photo essay of a lone Burr Oak thriving in southwest Wisconsin, shot entirely with an iPhone camera over the course of a year—one photo per day. The book is 192 pages, full color, 10x10 inches and may be purchased online by visiting:

www.thattree.net.

Previous Books by James C. Washburn

Touching Spirit: The Letters of Minominike

Table of Contents

Air

"To the East Where Father Sun rises Bringing to us a new day A new meaning of life, A light in which to see the path before us."
– Author L. Kibby

A Billion Fold

There on the edge of the trail lay a raven, her body still limp. Death had come recently. I picked her up and moved her alongside a mossy log. As I did the muted sounds of another could be heard. Above my head, in a white oak, sat what must have been her mate rocking back and forth as if for solace over the loss.

"Consider the birds of the air," One said long ago.

Sadly, most of modern humanity is too busy to "consider" any of our Relations. Most of modern humanity is cut off from creation, being surrounded by asphalt, noise and steel. We were created to play in the "Fields of the Lord," to hear the songs of insects, feel the embrace of cool soil around our toes, shiver in the wind and wonder at what is out there in the dark of night, threatening. The mystery and the passion of life is most profoundly felt away from the din of the urban world.

Artificial entertainment goes only so far in creating delight. Our art, as amazing as human creativity can be, is only a facsimile of what spontaneously erupts a billion fold every day in Creation.

I sat down a respectable distant from her body and looked his way. His eye glistened, head tilted, and he spoke a broken rasp. Yes, a sad and broken rasp.

If you question the existence of consciousness in our Relations you haven't spent enough time in their presence. The doors of Creation's temple are open. There is no fee to enter. Mystery and passion await you.

Think on Things Such as This

 Think on things such as this - It is claimed that our physical body entirely replaces itself over a period of seven years. Each of the 100 trillion cells from bone, skin, organs and muscle dies, is removed and replaced. The DNA, genes, proteins, the molecules and atoms that make up your every cell are scattered over the earth. That which was you is dispersed on the wind, into the rivers, seas and the soil. That which was you becomes grass, grain or leaf, deer, firefly, eel and raven.

If this is what you become, who have you been? The chances are good that the present, past and future components of many of your 100 trillion cells will have been at one time bison or sparrow, redwood, Leaf Erickson, Buddha or Jesus. You likely have or had molecules of Bantu, Arab, Cherokee, Norse, and surely part of the stars of the galaxy from which all elements have been born.

In more ways than I can imagine I am linked to all of creation. Not just allied, but intimately inseparable from everyone and all that is. You and I are interconnected, interdependent, interrelated. This is ultimate reality and thinking on things such as this inaugurates the birth of humility and respect. From humility grows wisdom and its supreme beauty - universal love. From respect grows peace, sorely needed in the mind of humankind.

This is the beginning of knowing creation as the Maker of All Things knows it. It is the beginning of your freedom from bondage to desperate self-preservation. Think on things such as this.

Ears to Hear

Drifting high in the night sky, ice particles muted the remnants of a waning moon. It was one o'clock in the morning and as is my habit before bedtime I had taken my seat on the floor before the frosted window. Here, with moon and stars suspended, I pretend to meditate. Here, most nights, I fight the screaming monkey in my head and make an attempt at mindfulness. It is here that I ponder and sometimes hold conversation with the Great Mystery. I have to admit the conversation is not a real dialogue. That requires two voices and the One to whom I make address I do not often perceive a response. This is because, like most, I rarely listen with ears to hear.

"Ears" that hear the Voice of Forever are not affixed on either side of our heads. No, they are attached to our hearts. The Voice, the Word, is not a word that comes from "out there." It is not the voice of mosque, temple, synagogue or church. You don't have to have an account, subscribe or be a member to "log in."

So, there I sat attempting to touch and impress the transcendent as if I had something to offer. It was there in the midst of this foolishness I "heard." What was said, you might ask? Are you ready for this?—Nothing!

The Voice of Forever cannot be confined to speech. It rises up from the eternal depth of Being which you contain but which even more contains you. Language is always deficient. Interpretation is always lacking. No tongue can sufficiently express what you've "heard." The "word" is not grasped so much as it grasps and seizes you. At best, all that can ever be stated about "hearing" is wrapped up in a four-letter word, LOVE. Incomprehensible, unbounded LOVE.

I lifted myself from the floor and ran a fingernail through the frost on the window. Nomadic clouds of ice still muted the thin sliver of moon in night sky. The universe, this planet, me, you, travel through the eternal ether of LOVE, the eternal Word.

You DO have ears to hear.

Consider the Parrot

I once knew a parrot named El Papagayo. He lived near Tamarindo, Costa Rica. We humans are classified in the order primate. I think we're more closely related to parrots.

Parrots can survive eighty years, like us. Some are omnivores, like us. I once saw El Papagayo eating a chili dog. They're intelligent, like we're supposed to be. Their brain to body ratio is similar to humans. They transmit knowledge across generations. No, they don't run public or private parrot schools, but they teach one another. They walk with a rolling gate like many of us. You should have seen El Papagayo waddling toward the dog when he was pissed off! Poor dog.

It's obvious—we humans are parrots without feathers. When in large groups they're unruly, bullying, destructive and they frick'n bite! Remind you of anyone? They're noisy and don't clean up after themselves. They recite to the command of their masters with little if any thought. See? Parrots without feathers—that's us!

However, the greatest similarity is in the way we both express ourselves. Let me rephrase that. It's in the way we "parrot" ideas. If you want to fly with the flock you've got to talk the talk. In the limiting "thought ghettos" of our personal worlds we're taught by people parroting what they were taught by people who parroted the parrots before them. You get the point. There's little room to squeak a different squawk.

However, trace a particular flock's "truth" far enough back and you end up with presumptions built upon assumptions based on conjectures. Pass that speculation down a few generations and you've got Truth with a capital "T", unchallengeable, unquestionable, unassailable, and God ordained. Such is the nature of "truth" more than we care to admit, especially in the religious realms.

When was the last time in the quiet of your heart you openly and honestly questioned, dissected, pondered, the validity of the paradigms you parrot to the world? To do so can be scary but the results can set you free.

El Papagayo had been programmed with a large vocabulary and he had a good life. He pleased his keepers. But, one day sighting a free and adventurous wild parrot, he became aware of the bondage of his existence and when he was forty-nine years old, the cage door opened and he took flight! Occasionally he can be seen soaring brilliantly near his previous home. He no longer mimics former voices to garner approval. Instead, in liberty he proclaims his own words to the world.

El Papagayo is a free bird.

A Dream

This is the story of a dream: Today, sitting on my porch out of the wind and with the sun warming my face, I began to doze off. As is common in fall, bees were seeking a hiding place for the upcoming cold season. Numerous models of these insect aircraft were hovering nearby, legs, like landing gear, dangling below, engine rpms at minimum.

As the curtains lowered over my eyes I fell into the dreamtime. There, in a parallel universe, robed in yellow and brown, a Cessna sized bee stood with flaps down, engine off. A phased array of lenses peered at me gathering information without a blink.

Drawn toward this craft I used one of its legs as a boarding step and perched myself atop the forward abdominal cabin. Jointed antennae snapped back, and I gripped the last segments. Liftoff! Maximum acceleration!

Instantly airborne we banked to the right and headed through the trees. In no time we reached elevation with rising vapors. At eleven o'clock sailed a lone swallow and ahead a family of grackles thrashed about in the turbulence of our wake as we flashed by. Fields, marshes, orchards passed below and suddenly a dizzying sharp decent brought us to a colony of white boxes.

Panic was rampant in this sweet-city as it seemed few workers had returned from a recent foray. A regal looking drone, colleague of my ride, approached and with twitching antennae, buzzed, dipped and nodded instructions for a mission. We turned, ambled to the edge of the hive and were off.

Stop after stop we discovered remains laced with the toxic pollen of insecticides, GMOs, fungicides. At each one my pilot lightly massaged the dead with the hairs of its own body picking up clues to report back to base. At each one my pilot seemed less coherent, less empowered for flight.

Finally, our flight plan fulfilled, we again approached the colony but this time gliding in on what little strength remained. The runway was clear. No permission-to-land was forthcoming from the silent tower. Our touchdown was rough and upon taxiing to a stop my friend collapsed among the bodies of the hive.

I startled from sleep to discover a wasp and bee having conversation on the back of my hand. They turned and looked in my direction. "You need us," they seemed to say. "Consider your ways."

Megwetch

Smoke rose toward overhanging branches as a long-handled pitchfork disturbed the embers. Twenty-eight cobble-sized "Grandfathers" of smooth glacial granite had been in the fire for over an hour and radiated impatience for the sweat lodge to begin. Respectfully, on hands and knees we entered a lone east-facing door circling a central depression in Mother Earth, men on one side, women the other. From the fire, seven times I am handed the fork holding a single Grandfather and in thanksgiving place them in the depression, "Boozhoo Mishomis" (welcome Grandfather).

A canvas door flap swings down and all is dark except for the warm ruby glow at our center. An aroma of sweet-grass and tobacco fills the lodge as a pipe is lit, smoked, and an offering of prayer ascends bringing silence and introspection.

Here, in this womb of safety you can look within to look beyond. Here, as we journey inside this ancient ceremony, solidarity grows while respect and companionship encircle our hearts.

A single drum sounds, sets the tempo and the first of four songs begins accompanied by shakers of turtle shell, gourd, rawhide. The temperature soars and breathing becomes heavy as water, showering from a branch of cedar, releases the wisdom of the Grandfathers. Condensed steam and sweat drip from my beard, run down my body, carry away the trivial and vain as I am forced to confront only the essentials of life. Discomfort increases, a reflection of our struggles and pain in this world.

Four times, seven Grandfathers are added to the already searing center of our lodge. Four times we embrace the sacred darkness to look within and look beyond.

Every lodge brings meekness to my soul and the realization of our need for grace in order to live, grace from our Creator and grace from one another.

Standing before the ashes where once twenty-eight Grandfathers rested I hold tobacco next to my heart and offer thanksgiving for all the experiences of life. At this moment, in focused awareness, I am attuned to the Presence within and without of my Father of Creation. From my heart my tongue softly speaks, "Megwetch," (thank you).

Night Walk

A dream had awakened me. Losing the battle to return to sleep I put on my clothes and stepped outside. Now, in another surreal dreamscape, before the moon surrendered the night to the sun, I ventured alone in a monochromatic world where my vision was opened to the unity before me. My state of reality altered, and I saw harmony in all things.

In the surf's roar and silent movement of mists, in every act of love and kindness, in the heart of Sequoia and every creeping thing is Spirit's habitation. She/he floats through grass and rides the whirlwind. She/he fashions ocean wave and chisels mountain crags. In the breath of Vesuvius and collapse of St. Helen, in the whispering grace of the lily, the Answer to All Mysteries is revealed. In you, in me, in friend and enemy, within sentient and inanimate dwells One Designer.

I looked into the sky and asked myself, "How is it that this Truth is so unmistakable, yet so often hidden? How is it that I should walk in blindness before the

Artist, deafness in the company of the Conductor, as zombie in the presence of Life?"

This knowledge of the heart is heaven itself. This knowing that we are immersed in the Great Caring, lifts us to wonder and holy carelessness, frees us to live.

Here in the divinity of this night I had fallen into this One Who is always there, my Beginning and My End, my Comfort, Peace and Lover. She/he is the fire in the forest and its rebirth from dark ash. She/he is in the beauty of tender compassion, in hunting wolf and broken bones of caribou, in Solomon's temple and the Pyramids of Giza.

Though we are often distracted, deceived, though, in fear we needlessly struggle for survival and approval, around us at every moment is our All Parent—Father/Mother, the Loving Anchor of Reality, and I, we, all things are safely, forever embraced.

In this night, now standing near a solitary elm whose umbrella like canopy sealed off the sky, it occurred to me—beyond what obscures my vision is that which is actual, that which transcends what I think so real.

My stroll in the night was not a dream, but a walk toward awakening.

Early in the Morning

I put my gear into the canoe and pushed away from shore. My momentum carried me out of the shadows into warm light. It was four in the morning and creation was stirring, beginning to find its voice. At this latitude the sun had been up for half an hour singing its life-giving energy into the sky. Clouds and mountain peaks, illuminated by horizontal light, were re-imaged on the lake's black water. Breath turned to vapor hanging beautifully before me as I disturbed a sleepy crowd of water scooters with the first stroke of my paddle. They followed and together we glided in virtual silence along the surface carrying our lives out into the soon awakening chorus of a new day. Only the soft sound of wood pulling water could be heard effortlessly moving our little parade toward the sand bar formed near the river's inlet.

The echo of this moving water had ushered me to sleep in the night. As we rounded the bar, there on the beach lay a cow moose and her calf. My scooter friends and I had startled her. Hackles were bristling, ears back. They arose, and mom stepped into the water as her gangly calf, maybe two months old, curiously peeked under her belly.

Only twenty-five yards apart and in shallow water, I got ready to head out into the deep. She was ready to fight. My scooter friends and I were no match for an 800-pound moose. Thankfully, she blew a snort through her nose and moved sideways over a windfall. Stepping into the brush she kept her eyes focused on the threatening intruders.

Her toddler, although alerted to danger, was overtaken with interest and stayed watching, initiating an interspecies dialog between mom, calf, my entourage of six legged escorts and myself. Our conversation consisted of ear twitches, a stiffening here and there of muscles, questioning bleats. My scooters bobbed up and down sharing whatever passed through their nano-sized brains. As the only human present I chimed in with pleasantries about the morning followed up with flattery. A Steller Jay landed at the bar, placed an order, and sipped from the lake. Sounding somewhat inebriated he offered a raucous comment and left for the far shore.

At that moment we "heard" another voice, a voice whispering in the language of spirit. We—human, moose, scooters, all that is, is sustained by the command of this speech. It is the voice that gives form and consciousness, the voice of being, the voice of harmony, sustaining creation in communion.

Now, having been gracefully granted "ears to hear," we became silent before the eternal Word as the illusion of our otherness evaporated. This mystical "sound", this awareness of the oneness of reality, is there for all to "hear."

I cannot say how long this spiritual union lasted, this high state of pure being. A breeze began tugging at the bow and as my physical senses imposed their control I moved the paddle into the water for stability. Still, I was overcome with peace beyond understanding as we parted ways.

Gliding over the reflection of the world I knew the echoes of this place would stay with me forever.

Trust the Wind

"The wind blows where it wills, you hear the sound thereof, but cannot tell from where it came or know where it goes."

As I turned and walked toward the sun, pondering these ancient words, the soft caress from a northeast breeze lightly washed the side of my face. Now and then a dandelion seed drifted past carried along tethered below its fragile parachute.

It was a heavenly morning bathed in the smells of blossoming cherries and crab apples.

A kingbird joined me and flew alongside the gravel road, landing every ten yards or so to see if I was keeping up. He considered himself my guide for quite a while until suddenly I instinctively ducked as something glided past my eyes. Turning to look I caught sight of a small floating sphere, brown and gray, hardly the size of a dried pea. I reversed directions and zeroed in on this odd mystery.

It was a spider curled upside-down and hanging unto the thinnest of filaments being played out vertically from between its legs. Tending the length of the filament she carefully regulated the height and speed of her wind born adventure. My eyes followed this ultra-thin fiber of silk upward five, ten, fifteen feet until it nearly disappeared out of sight.

A current of air met us from around a grove of trees and wafted my aeronautical friend out into the field. I jumped the ditch to keep up. Ahead grew a collection of shrubs maybe eight feet tall. I thought, for sure, her journey was about end, but no!

Working legs feverishly, higher and higher my tiny Earhart ascended clearing all entanglements. Clearly no amateur, no Icarus experimenting with wax and feathers, I became convinced I was watching Peter Parker wholly transformed.

Onward she flew, this intrepid traveler of the wind, with me riding shotgun on the ground. A hundred yards ahead stood the forest and ridge that restricted the Little Eau Pleine River into a series of rapids.

Working the gossamer filament my ballooning friend began to slow as if to study the challenge standing between it and continued freedom. She waited, bobbed up and down, floated forward, backwards. Suddenly her enthusiastic response began, legs and spinnerets were summoned to action. It was as if she was waiting, sensing pressures and direction for the perfect airstream.

Sure enough, what can only be described as a genius beyond human comprehension, she was lifted up and up and up as the Spirit of the Wind fanned my brave sky sailor onward into the unknown.

Spirit's "wind blows where it wills," Jesus said. My small friend had shown me her faith to trust in the ride.

Grise Fiord, Nunavut

 Like an enormous parasol, a cloudless dazzling sky arched above me. Leaving the rocky slope behind I continued upward on the snow and ice. Now at over 1,000 feet above the Arctic Ocean the sun's reflected glare brought my pupils to their smallest aperture possible. I turned away from the brilliance, pulled dark goggles from my pack and slipped them over my eyes. In a few minutes crampons with one-inch claws were secured to my boots and I ascended the glacier higher into the blue.

Sweat began to build under my coat and hat. I lashed them to the pack. The silence was absolute. No movement of air. The only sound, blood pumping through my ears, labored breathing.

Finally, my second wind kicked in and it felt like I could continue upward, surmounting the very throne room of God. Around me photons of color filled my vision as microscopic crystals of ice refracted light. Step after step, higher and higher.

Overcoming a drift of crusted snow, I approached the final terrace of ice. Now on hands and knees I drove the toe claws of my crampons into the steep slope. Slivers of ice clattered downward through the still air. I leaned forward and pressed my body against the chill before the final rise.

Slowly the angle reduced and before me loomed the edge of the world. I had conquered the climb. In the stillness, the crushing silence, I pushed my head over the granite lip. There 1300 feet below, tiny winged profiles soared above the still frozen ocean. I looked away, dizzy, unsteady and hugged the stone I lay upon.

At that moment, in this northern world of blue, white and grey, sky, snow, and stone, I was stripped of pretense and pride, forced to confront the raw and humbling truth of my frailty. It is only by grace, pure and simple, that I exist at all. Only by grace that I am allowed the illusion of my dominion over life, and by an even greater grace I am brought back from the edge of arrogance to humility and gratitude. The conceit of my self-importance, my power, the deception of control, was driven out of the shadows by the light of a higher consciousness. As my ego struggled to return to the helm, to conjure again the smoke and mirrors of its dark magic, into the air my lips uttered simply, "thank you for my existence."

A tulugaq (raven) perched itself atop the cliff to my left. I smiled in appreciation to the Great Mystery for speaking to me. The iridescent bird croaked a bit of advice and with abandon leaped into the void. I turned and in meekness began my descent.

Raven

 For three nights he had been my escort in the dreamtime. I follow him in soundless flight, take in his raven eye view, merge with his thoughts, dark thoughts, probing, revealing the ways and whys of human behavior.

"You take pride in your self-consciousness, yet you are unconscious of all but yourself. Your kind is alienated from your home and the voice of creation resounding the divine is silent. In separating yourself from intimacy with the grandeur and mystery of the greater world you diminish meaning within your inner world. Return to the scriptures of creation, know our common origin and destiny, feel the warm life-giving care and embrace of our loving Creator and be at rest."

For three nights in the dark I awoke, sat on the edge of my bed and wondered at the words of my escort. We are not separate from creation but an integral part of the universe. The pathology of our culture's materialism feeds the virus of greed, destroys creation and strangles the spiritual, leaving us without meaning.

Then, there, in the early morning of the fourth day, he sat alone. There, on the corner post of the garden he watched, surveying horizon and field. He was larger than most, clearly aged. He held himself with dignity crafting an aura of wisdom. Seesawing over the fulcrum of his legs he cawed and waited, cawed and waited. I stepped outside onto the porch. He fixed his black raven eye to mine and would not let go. Only the gentle toss of a stone separated us and in that space between his eye and mine came these paraphrased words of old, "Consider the raven. They do not sow or reap or hoard things away, and yet God gives them plenty of what they need. Are not you as important in Creator's eyes?"

With that he sprang upward and the rush of air from his wings was felt on my face. He banked between white pine and birch, let his caw be heard and was gone.

He is no longer my escort in the dreamtime, yet the words from long ago are with me, echoing, ringing their truth and rest in my heart.

A Triangulation of Consciousness

 Walking on a fog filled morning, I stooped low to keep from disturbing branches laden heavy with drizzle. Not low enough. A cold shower found its way down the back of my neck, each drop laughing as it slid beneath my collar.

In this posture of humility, closer to the earth, I picked up the scent. I had heard a thin snort ahead in the fog several minutes before and slowed my pace, tweaked my senses. The musk raised my head slowly to scan the brush, watch for the slightest movement.

She stomped the ground with a front hoof. My eye instantly zeroed in, but she was not solely fixed on me. Instead, her ears and eyes trained slightly to my east. There, Ma'iingan (wolf) with his alpha-companion. In this interspecies standoff, this triangulation of consciousness, our awareness focused onto this singular moment. Each of us puzzled at the intentions of the other, intrigued, alert, weighing responses. Each of us in catatonic like state, creating a memory field that would be accessible for the rest of our existence.

Initial mistrust dissolved into the fog as thousands of generations of ancestors stood looking through our eyes into the eyes of one another. My tension and pulse slowed, as did the same in wolf and deer. A slow blink, tilt of head, a wag of tail, and lowering of standing shoulder hair spoke between us that we shared the graces of life.

From my experience there is no higher state, no greater joy than a momentary glimpse of our connectedness, our unity with creation and the Great Mystery of Creator. This oneness, best described in terms of love, binds and fuses all beings and things in the phenomena of existence.

Heavy fog again drifted between us veiling our union. Through it I was gifted with a final glimpse of my relations withdrawing into the mist. The corners of my mouth and eyes turned upward as several more drops found their way down the back of my neck. I continued my journey.

Grayness

 Ascending, just above the threshold of visibility, perceived more with imagination than certainty, a golden thread rose from beyond the horizon uniting earth to heaven. Half still in the dreamtime, I squinted through the branches where in morning darkness I had made my nest. Eastward, the goddess Eos stirred and her hoped for warmth contrasted sharply with the chill around and in me. Waif-like vapors, released from the jacket of frost over the ground, began their skyward climb, drawing my soul with them.

I had come here seeking a glimpse, a touch, a taste of what again was real. The ease and affluence of contemporary living had siphoned off the fire, smoothed out the edges and hardships of life, causing my descent into self-absorption. It seems only a measure of physical struggle with primal forces begets appreciation and meaning. The vitality of the universe itself springs from this warfare and tension.

As I sat motionless, focused on realigning my heart with life, movement near a frozen puddle caught my eye like a magnet. They darted onto the ice, two mink in winter dress. Twisting, leaping, clinging to one another in excited dance, the radiance for life these relations gave out was palpable. These hyperactive weasels exuded joy itself. It was against their nature not to.

From open mouths rapid puffs of breath exhausted into the cold air until they played themselves out, collapsing on the frost in each other's arms. The corners of my mouth turned up and inside, my heart again warmed.

Grayness will afflict us all, some with darker shades than others. In cold twilight hopeful vision is limited. This morning I surmised Creator had directed these relations my way. They brought the medicine I needed.

As that golden thread pulled up the morning sun I left my nest with renewed anticipation to live.

Vapors of a Dream

The vapors of a dream lingered as I made my way to the window. Far off in the east, lightning from a local storm sought release in reaching for the earth. The flash of this dream was gone but its rumble in my subconscious could still be felt. It was as if—from somewhere in the obscure depths of my being—someone yearned to be heard, freed, discharged into the world.

I laced my boots, slipped on my jacket and stepped into the damp twilight. Overhead a nighthawk sang and followed my path down the gravel road. Only the slow roll of distant thunder intruded upon the calm of this evening. Here I was, walking alone in the coming darkness, yet, this someone, this visitor from the dream lingered nearby seeking recognition.

I stopped, turned, looked upward to the curtain of clouds in the sky and a realization became clear. The someone of my dream, all the "someones" of my dreams, are one and the same. The voice yearning to be heard, freed, discharged into the world was my true self. The drifter, this image, this nomad within, was my original face. Before the imprinting of conventions and habits, before the indoctrinations of culture, before fear and selfishness, before enslavement to self-judgment, this being existed.

Standing there on the gravel, lightning far in the east, it was as though I realized for the first time the nobility of my original face and that of all beings. Not the apparitions we present to the world or the hallucinations we buy into about ourselves and others, but the intrinsic beauty of being, the elemental virtue and divinity of which all partake.

As I continued my walk I listened more intently to the low voice of thunder speaking from beyond my view and my nighthawk companion resumed her strange electric like cries in the darkening sky.

Fire

"To the South where the warm air comes to us
Bringing heat and warmth,
The seasons of spring and summer."
—L. Kibby

Trinity and The Cur

A first snow has lightly sprinkled the forest floor not too many miles from Eagle River. Progressing through the Hemlock one silent step at a time, I'm drawn to a calamity heading my way from the east. Into the silence breaks a bobcat being chased by a burly mixed breed cur three times her size. She had had enough and came to a sudden stop near a dead-fall.

Remember the scene in *The Matrix* where Carrie-Anne Moss, aka Trinity, floats in the air and dispatches her pursers as the camera does a 360 of the fight scene? I think this bobcat saw the movie. The Cur, speeding full tilt in for the kill, compressed his body like an accordion against the dead-fall, nose fusing with bark. Above him floated Carrie-Anne, hair on end, claws extended, eyes gleefully filled with anticipation of the soon to commence ride. Down onto The Cur's back she came and hung on.

First there was the canine's squeal as sixteen talons took a grip. Next began the dance of the Islamic Sufi—the Whirling Dervish. Never was there a religious ceremony of this intensity ever performed. Round and round he spun but Carrie-Anne would not be displaced. Eyes growing more desperate with each turn he tries rolling the queen from her throne of torture. From my position as voyeur she was clearly riding butch in this sadomasochistic bedlam.

Up on his feet and in my direction The Cur bolted. Not more than ten yards off Carrie-Anne apparently decided the rodeo ride had gone on long enough. Three paws released their grip but retracting the talons on foot number four was not as easy. Dangling on one side of The Cur, bouncing, flopping and hissing until almost in my lap her predicament ended as she tumbled against a stump.

The Cur, a stone's throw away, stood making an odd mixture of sounds—snarls, whines and whimpers. The rider par excellence, panting, kept shaking foot number four trying to dislodge the chunks of hide pulled from the canine's flank.

They stared. They drooled. The inner sounds diminished. They stared some more. Eventually— silence. The forest was calm after a hurricane of madness. Casually, each turned away and left for home as if to say, "was it as good for you as it was for me?"

Fire in Our Eyes

I once had a friend who inherited a young dog from his elderly mother. Chofshi was a fun loving, chase the ball and cat, pee on your tires, dig up the garden fellow. My friend set about to form Chofshi into his image of what dog-ness should be.

To make a long story short, after a few months of testing, demanding discipline, punishment and various behavior modification techniques Chofshi was now the perfect dog. Perfect - in my neighbor's eyes.

He no longer jumped, spun around, wagged his entire rear end, stuck his nose in embarrassing places, or smiled from his heart. Love for life's adventures was drained from his eyes as he spent his days on the end of a chain being "good."

He had fresh water, decent food and as long as he remained muted he would even get a head pat now and then. The real Chofshi, however, begged for liberty.

He spent seven years on that chain. One day my friend was transferred and this dispirited hair bag became mine. I live in the country - no need for the chain. I own a shovel. I can fill in holes. Balls? Who knows where over two dozen have gone? His nose once again probes embarrassing places, and, hundreds of gallons of pee have not damaged my tires! It took time, but his gift of life was again released. Chofshi, by the way, is Hebrew for "free, not bound, unconstrained."

At birth we are unbounded innocent curiosity, filled with adventurous desires, creative exuberance. There is fire in our eyes and lust for life, imputed and running over from our being. However, for most, the chains come early. We are told life is a test with eternal consequences. It's pass or fail and the "Eye of Sauron" looms over our path.

This is a lie. We are not under cosmic examination to determine our worth. The gaze of Creator reflects joyous celebration and delight, dancing over you and me. Everyone is born a Chofshi, at liberty to follow your heart. Free from liability in order to swim in the experiences of existence. Free to make mistakes, suffer. Free to again "re-joy-ce", gain wisdom and resume the adventure.

Chofshi passed on a while back. His spirit is surely chasing a cat or digging a hole. I imagine God is hosing off the tires on the car.

Serenity and Fearsomeness

The atmosphere filled with gold as light forced its way between the wind-driven clouds, low in the western sky. I reached with cupped hands and drew the Spirit of this air onto my face. The windows through which I imagined the scene became steamy with gratitude. Here was the tangible presence of God.

Where do we find wonder and awe? How is the spirit of humankind astonished, uplifted? From where does the divine spark flare out and cause you to marvel?

I pondered this as I knelt in the fallen leaves secretly watching a family of Teal dabbling the surface of a small back bay. Here in this protected cove the thought occurred to me, if I could say anything to the universe it has to be, "Thank you."

The downside of technology, power and urbanization has been the isolation of modern man from what is real, from what is transcendent. We are starved for the Creative Presence. Our capacity to experience the sublime in creation is being lost as the virtual world of the artificial dominates our lives. In your center you know this to be true.

Shadow flashed across the water and the Teal family was startled to attention. Osprey was on the wing, an airborne glider with talons hunting in the gold. This family of six scurried to the reeds, hidden and safe while colored leaves, sailboat like in the sky, floated on the wind above them.

Here was wonder and amazement at the perfection of Creation's complex workings. It was here, within Creation's garden of serenity and fearsomeness, within the mysteries and questions, that the ecstasy of awe was first birthed in the heart of humankind. There is a mystical component to our being. We were fashioned to inhabit the golden light of God's magnificent splendor portrayed in creation.

Bend a knee in the temple of the universe and childlike astonishment will rise again. This shall be your praise.

Night Fires

 Here and there among the ashes of the evening fire, a small flame brightened the night as my stick stirred the remaining coals. I slipped my pipe into its leather pouch. It was past midnight. Time to begin threading my way home across the meadow under night skies.

Millennia after millennia we gathered around the night fires, absorbed their radiation, and gazed upward into eternity. Drawn together around the soft glow and dancing embers, night whispered mysteries to our human family of long ago. There we mused over the day as darkness tenderly pulled us toward introspection. The sun may have scattered our souls, stretched them over of the land, but Cassiopeia, Polaris, Orion and our fires returned us to our center. It was the splendor, the patterns and power of that black dome that brought us again to our humility. It was fire that kept the terror of the night away. In the light of our fires, a light swallowed by the overwhelming heavens, we understood our frailty. Hundreds of thousands mystical nights and fires are imprinted on our genetic memory. Our conscious initiation into the divine came through baptism in those night fires of the past.

To know your place in the world, the roots of your being, sit in the night. Tend the fire in silence and meekness. Look within and above. Feel the magnitude of your insignificance and the immeasurable value of your uniqueness. The catalyst of night fire, the flicker of stars, still turn our heart in amazement toward the loving gaze and embrace of the Architect of the Universe.

For the soul's wisdom, flee the toxic lights of mercury, neon and sodium. Turn from the glare. Peer into the coals of low fire and endless sky. Know that you are being observed and understood. You are not alone. Go into the frightening majestic night, light your fire and listen to our ancestors softly speak, "there is nothing to fear."

Leaving the meadow and stepping onto gravel road I again removed my pipe from its leather pouch. In the silence I rekindled a tiny red glow in its bowl, offering fragrance into the air around me. Night-bird hooted in the east as if calling up the moon not yet risen. The distant past was walking with me and starlight would guide me home.

No Partiality

An ethereal world lay before me. Early morning light was diffused. Visibility, 200 feet at best. The sound of flowing water called me into the mist and as I drifted through the fog each breath inhaled a cold stream of humidity. Our first snow lay upon the leaves and grass, hung from the trees, and slipped off branches at the behest of gravity.

Gravity! Its Law will not be violated.

At the edge of the river beneath the thin white layer, unknown to me laid a shed branch, slippery, without bark. The steep bank, lubrication of melting snow, and that inviolable Law united to have their way.

The temporal area of my head hit first followed by the rest of my carcass. I will not repeat the words, motivated by pain, which immediately filled the air. Thereupon came the buzzing, drowning out all other peaceful sounds of that sublime morning. A dark tunnel squeezed itself around my vision and my present level of consciousness was gone.

Flying into that tunnel came colors and light, iridescent and translucent, metallic and phosphorescent, each singing their personalities to the accompanying white noise.

A shaking and trembling awakened me. My body was entering hypothermia and reacted by shivering violently. I must have been there a half hour, legs soaking up the cold river I had slipped into. I pulled myself higher onto the bank raising feet onto a stone to allow the water to drain from my boots. I had to get up, move, generate heat. As I stood the change in circulation stabbed my attention to the side of my head. Everything seemed intact despite the pain. It was a half-mile to get back home, drink something warm.

Working hard climbing out of the river valley the violent shivering stopped. Even my legs heated up.

Creation is not partial to our species. She does not play favorites or cut us any slack. "We live and move and have our being" humbly in the universe.

The haunting beauty of this unforgettable morning could have been my last. Even so, I embrace the experience. I accept the pain. I will not hesitate to venture forth tomorrow or the next. I cherish the opportunity of existence.

Appreciation for the gift of life is expressed in its full use, to the extent we are capable. Preservation and longevity is not its goal. Pain and risk, pleasure and discovery, are interwoven in the adventure.

Your life awaits you.

Yesterday

 Yesterday I built a fort of sticks and tall grass, invincible, secure against giants and monsters. Yesterday I watched a beetle abandon a dispute with a bumblebee, and went fishing with my dad. I saw a fawn nursing. Perched from a high branch I launched walnuts and spit onto my friends below, jumped on my bed until a spring broke. Yesterday I ran through the field until I couldn't breathe, then fell into the alfalfa staring at the clouds. Yesterday my Grandpa died, then my Grandma, then the suicides of my friends after Vietnam and I buried my dog. Yesterday I got married, had a daughter, adopted a son, watched them build forts, study bugs, jump on their beds, become better educated than I.

Walking by a storefront window yesterday I saw the reflected image of a slower moving, graying man. In the background, fused hand-in-hand, was a string of excited children on a daycare field trip—faces with large absorbing eyes, mouths jabbering with elation.

Maybe they had just seen a wise beetle or a hungry fawn.

Wrapped in yesterdays, our lives, our memories are carried with us into tomorrow and become the sweet "thank you" we offer to forever.

With abandon, take up your adventure in soul making! That is the reason God grants the journey of life. Tomorrow, I think I'll go outside and build a fort of sticks and grass, try and climb a tree, help my wife take a walk.

Spring of '67

Something across the meadow, a fleeting movement inside the brush, caught my attention. Stepping silently back into the shadows I stood motionless waiting for my eyes to adjust. Was I being watched? By whom, what? My eyes focused, dissected the shapes, colors. Inside my chest my heart responded to the adrenalin brought on by the unknown. I felt its pulse in my neck. All seemed natural, ordinary, as the mysterious life form remained hidden. I needed patience and slowly leaned against the birch behind me.

Two minutes, five, ten passed. A chickadee, pondering my catatonic state, darted within reach and began a monologue. Soon two colleagues appeared, and this tribunal commenced deliberation as to the meaning of this human fused to the tree.

"Imagine that - a human that has ceased to thrash about in our home." The first seemed to say.

"Why isn't it making noise or hauling off parts of our world?" Mused a second.

"Don't trust it. Don't get too close. It might be a trap!" The third repeated over and over.

At one point, to the shock and horror of the third member of the trinity, the first rushed in and snatched a deer fly from the brim of my cap, removed the wings and enjoyed a snack.

To my right a downy woodpecker impatiently considered a fissure in the bark as if waiting for fast food at the drive up.

All around me the show continued. Ants in single file ascending/descending the birch I leaned against, an unfurling fiddlehead stretched skyward as if waking from a nap and there, half buried, an acorn had broken out of its case sending tender yellow root downward and slender diminutive brown stalk with two tiny leaves toward heaven.

Suddenly, the mystery was revealed. A high-pitched snort came from across the way. There she was with two fawns, eye's fixed on her. Her eyes fixed on me. A hoof abruptly striking the earth shot the little ones into the brush. She turned and with a single leap followed, tail flagging white. Only an occasional rustle and crack revealing their route.

It was the spring of '67. Today I visit this meadow, now covered with asphalt, to buy unessential items of vanity. There is no longer mystery here, no brother/sister creatures, no sedges, rushes, no birch. Today barren hardness surrounds me mixed with unyielding noise. I step up onto the curb as my eyes are attracted to an idyllic poster of Creator's earth and I question the folly of "progress".

Creator's WMD

 I left the tent flap open to catch what little breeze there was. It was a hot, humid, moonlit July night and I lay with my head at the door absorbing the quiet. This canvas antique leaked mosquitoes even more than rain. Still, I figured it would serve to keep out possum, coon and skunks.

Wait, I have to be dreaming. Aren't dreams in black and white? Eight inches from my face, curling up his dime sized nose at what obviously was the repulsive stench of a human three days without a shower, was a young polecat.

"Lay still." I told myself. "No fast moves."

Luckily his business end was aimed the other way, but I sensed he was priming it. He came closer. I remained mute, catatonic, eyes slowly crossing as his twitching sniffer pushed the tent screen to my forehead. There was no back door.

Then I saw it, a virtual invasion, a battalion of black fur with racing stripes, shadows in the moonlight picking their way toward my flimsy, hopefully skunk proof bunker. It was a foray for worms and grubs by every Oreo with legs and tail in the county.

I kept my wits intact trying to control the thumping in my chest. The forward scout emitted a cackling squeak signaling four more troop members to my door and it dawned on me—maybe we could negotiate?

My first quiet syllable was clearly misunderstood, inducing an instant salute from each tail. Clearly the safeties were off, weapons cocked. This didn't seem like a good idea. I invited God to intervene and went back to playing dead.

Slowly the artillery was lowered and the summoned four returned to hunting in the soft wet humus. Only the original remained.

The sound of probing, scratching, overturning of leaves and sticks moved through the forest and downhill toward the creek. Yet, my first contact stayed as if glorying in his telekinetic power keeping me pinned to the floor of my tent. When the brigade could no longer be heard he headed off in overdrive to catch up, mission accomplished.

A slight bouquet of musk mingled with the damp ground. I lay relieved, even contented. Breathing easy, I mused of our encounter and the humor of Creator in devising this WMD. As I returned to sleep and dreams,

only the sound of moonlight flowing through the
branches filled the night

Trio

 Like a wave washing over sand, notes splashed through the forest around me. After a momentary silence again they came, clear and pure, filling my ears with song. Here was a celebration of life not to be denied.

I zeroed in on the source. There! A silhouette against the sky arching his neck upward, opening his mouth to declare, "I am! I am! I delight that I am!" His maple perch had been transformed to a dais of jubilation and from it with unreserved glee poured his existence. "I am! I am! I delight that I am," he proclaimed to the world.

From a distant part of the woods came the warble of another, an aria as filled with life as this Pavarotti above me. Then to my surprise a third, perhaps Carreras or Bocelli, completed the trio of praise.

I stood silently, closed my eyes and imagined even the Great Composer caught up in the joyful song of these lives. Glorious singing rolled through the air and rose to the attention of angles. Standing there in the eternal now of that moment they lifted the essence of my being in praise as well. "I am! I am! I delight that I am!" was drawn from my heart.

I pressed my forehead against the maple feeling it's life, enjoying this glorious thankfulness and the concord of our hearts. With that our quartet sensed another voice rising around us. "You are! You Are! I delight that you are!" It was the voice of Creator singing over His work. He, we, all our relations, distinct yet one choir in concert with the harmony of existence.

Today, now, sing the hymn, "I am! You are! We are! He delights in His Creation!" Let your tongue join the refrain, your ears hear the melody and dignity of all His work. This is the song of God.

Uncharted

The sky opened and for days Mother earth drank in the soothing rain. Showers from heaven refreshed the spirit of every plant, washed away the dust, purified the air. Humus, over saturated, could hold no more and shed the excess. I had portaged my canoe around the falls, overland to this spot. Standing under a hemlock I eavesdropped on the sound of rivulets trickling downhill into the river steadily increasing its flow. What once lazily spilled along the gentle slope meandering toward the great sea far away, was now hastening swiftly toward its resting place. The rushing torrent swelled and overcame all resistance. The flow, unstoppable.

In our youth we swim upstream, do battle with the tides and win. The River of Time spills out slowly before us. When floods swell, we confidently fight the surge and pretend to conquer their waves behind the illusion of our immortality. Yet, the river flows on.

Now and then, floating along were plants and shrubs torn from their hold on life. Catching the bank or a rock they momentarily resisted the onward rush.

This metaphor before me, this River of Life and Time, spoke to me loud and clear. I am being carried with increasing speed and I cannot resist its flow. My life, like yours and all our relations is moving inescapably to the great sea. The life I live rides this fast river like all life before and all to come.

As I stood there on the bank my eagerness to run this water flooded my heart with passion. An inner zeal to fully experience my privilege of existence eclipsed my hesitancy. What lies downstream can only be known by shooting the rapids, banging the hull here and there, taking on some water.

I kneeled on the ribs and launched into the current ready for the ride. Skirting a standing wave, I slipped into the channel yielding myself to what was to come. A sharp pivot around a ledge brought me into a sudden pitch and my speed increased down the chute. Nearly spilling, I pulled a hard draw stroke to the left and the curler at the bottom washed over the bow. A hundred more meters and I slid into an eddy to rest, bail water and savor my journey thus far.

Our voyage is a sacred adventure molding the soul. I often wonder at the excitement and danger, the joy and pain. Let us not hesitate on our holy voyage. What distance remains to the shore of the great sea I do not know, for my river, like yours, has no charts.

Through the Storm

A cold fierce wind bit hard upon our bodies. We looked for deliverance from its rage by heading downhill toward the ice-covered river. Here, within the crevice of a boulder and drifting snow we nested ourselves. Overhead air currents blasted through hemlock and leaf bare poplar, giving voice to the storm's wrath.

Pressing with me into this cleft of the rock was my hairy friend tail tucked tight, ears alert. Two species joined in common need. Horizontal snow corkscrewed in the eddy of our shelter, falling over man and dog like a gleaming blankct being tucked in by an invisible hand. Wrapped in Earth Mother's insulation, a warm presence began to envelop our beings. A mysterious peace beyond understanding settled upon our sanctuary as the chaos and frenzy continued. Fused with my companion in this serene state we sat joyful amidst the riot and watched the vapors of our breath rise and swirl out of sight.

Storms, mad hurricanes of pain, are inevitable. They rise slowly or blindside us without warning, taking our breath away. The pain brought our way by these tempests is part of the privilege of existence, the price of wisdom, the chisel shaping our souls.

My friend and I had hoped to make it back to our cabin before it came upon us. Our plans and hopes were not to be our lot. Yet, here in the midst of our distress, a retreat, both physical and spiritual, brought us solace and peace. Here in the cleft of the rock we found sanctuary. The rock of our refuge gave us consolation, weathering the trials with us.

Slowly the blanket thickened until it seemed we had been consumed. But, to the contrary, we rested content, safe within the storm. With the passing of time we emerged, man and dog, giving thanks for the experience, knowing our lives were more complete because of it.

My friend has long since passed on but I feel someday, beyond the western door, we will meet to recall the shaping of our souls on that cold day.

The Chaos of My Mind

The day had been hot and hectic. To find reprieve from heat and solace for my mind I walked to the river. Sweat covered my face attracting a deer fly to orbit my cap. I settled onto a ledge of granite with toes dangling in the amber water. She circled again and again unable to decide where to land. The cool rising boil in this stream gave me the relief I sought. Its hypnotic upwelling pulled my consciousness into the darkness and time stopped. The whys and wherefores of life that relentlessly course through my head vanished and the peace of pure existence was mine.

My frenetic companion slowed and came to rest on my hand. Together we listened, smelled, felt the privilege of being, and surveyed our moment in time. I licked the dried salt from my lips as she did from the back of my hand.

In the waters before us an image appeared, ancient, primitive, fundamental, eliciting the awareness of our bond to all that had gone before, to all that would follow. In the trance and rapture of these few minutes an appreciation for life was rekindled.

A sudden gust of wind moved downstream, and my friend launched herself from my hand whirling, spiraling once again around my cap. Like my companion, seemingly unable to touchdown, I sensed the chaos of my mind coiled nearby waiting to crawl back in on this hot and hectic day.

End of Eden

Pillows of grey dust ascended with each step, sticking to legs, clinging to sides and backs. Ghostlike they threaded their way through the ash, moving downhill toward the stream hoping to find reassurance that the annihilation of what once was home was not absolute.

Hungry man had been here, in Eden, reaping profit with howling, screaming machines. Driven by unending appetite, it was not enough to take only what was needed. This landscape of perfection upon which the sacred cycles of life, death, and life reborn, had for eons played out, was now consumed by black fire on the altar of man's discontent.

At the head of a ravine, aside granite boulder they halted, searching, smelling, unleashing a bark, then a whimper, in hopes that the Observer of All Things might intercede in this nightmare. Only silence responded.

In their garb of ashes and grief they pressed against each other waiting. There, in the center of a vast zone of war, after the terror had moved on in search of other victims, there in this once holy and serene home of a multitude now silent, they collapsed. The nearby former stream of life carrying away all hope.

Wind moved up the slope swirling cinders and debris and brought several dark winged watchers with it. They alighted on the boulder, looked down with cocked heads and catching the eyes of the grieving pair lifted off pulling these grey ghosts with them toward the ridge. In mournful gait they angled left then right making a slow alternating diagonal rise above the desolation. The last spirits to flee, they surmounted the climb and paused leaving their silhouette against the sky etched in the eye of my memory forever. Their family and Eden destroyed through the violence of our selfishness.

I stowed the binoculars and swung the pack over my shoulder. No smile crossed my face or raised the corners of my mouth. I turned to follow the trail back. Sadness and shame filled my heart as grey dust ascended behind me.

Dark Season

I drift down this path under cold cloud-covered skies. It is the lean time, a season of scarcity. My soul starves in the grayness. It is easier to live with a deficit of food than walk through life without meaning. The solstice has past yet darkness in my mind lingers. Time slips away, disappears in the short days and as the reality of my impermanence becomes clear, what I once was sure I knew is exposed as mere illusion.

I long for the shining stories and myths of childhood, the security of a warm lap, to be tucked into bed and told all is well, to wake up in the night and look forward to the adventures of tomorrow. Instead, menacing pointlessness stalks my thoughts. I find solace only in the grace to believe this is the privilege of being human—to experience the abandonment of meaning in order to throw one's self unto the mercy of a benevolent universe and in faith go forward.

This is the paradox that births ultimate meaning. Meaning and its peace, lie not in the self-confidence of our convictions or knowledge, but in the grace bestowed gift of faith in the midst of our struggle to understand. Seasons of darkness beset us all, bring suffering, coldness and clouds, depression.

With dull eyes I tread wearily down this path, a member of the walking dead. Where will it lead? When will it end? It is a forced march, a forward plodding in hope that out of this death, around the next corner resurrection will come into view.

There are those for whom the journey is too dark and end their traveling. I judge not. For me and hopefully for you should you be on this path under cold cloud-covered skies, history tells me spring will come. Walk on, for meaning may be just around the next corner.

Raven and Bear

Merging from violet to plum, the western horizon faded toward night. I banked the fire against the stone's face, put down a canvas, lay back and moved peacefully toward sleep. With the crackle of pitch to my side, soft earth below, clear vault of heaven above, how much more could I ask of Creator? The privilege of existence swept over my soul and I drifted into dreamtime.

Raven was first to call. With her dark eye penetrating my defenses she seized my inner self and drew me skyward. I looked down upon my body left behind, fragile, helpless, molded by experiences. A vessel of beauty—gifted and cherished by Creator, a treasure despite my hypocrisy, poor choices, judging, and cunning of my selfishness.

Suddenly out of the forest a bear (great medicine) approached my camp, head swaying side to side. Hot breath and drool flowing from its gaping mouth. Alders and spruce parted before him. Hanging above the scene, terror enveloped me. The bruin paused over my body, inspecting, evaluating and then as muscles rippled, stood upright, tilted its head toward me in the sky and spoke. "I gave you mercy. Will you do the same for others?"

Drenched and shivering in cold sweat I awakened to darkness, poked the fire and added some tinder. A spark ascended. Following it upward I located Ursa Major, the Great Bear of the night sky and the words of my dreamtime visitor returned. "Mercy," echoed through my mind all that night. Mercy, a concept of little import in the Darwinian social and economic systems at play in the world today, a concept driven into the corner by ego. Those who walk this earth at higher levels of consciousness are easily spotted by the mercy pouring forth from their lives. It is the hallmark of enlightenment.

A rasp startled me just before dawn. Alighting on her throne high among white spruce cones, her dark eye seemed to again penetrate the inclinations of my being. From earliest memories, these two, Raven and Bear, have haunted my dreams, shadowed my conscious life and even taken up residence, tattooed on my body. In ways I do not understand, the power of their introspective gaze is my continual companion.

Stirring the coals of a now dead fire I packed my canvas and began moving toward the morning light. I whispered a prayer of gratitude from a heart reminded of the mercy that grants me the privilege of existence. Leaving her throne on high, Raven also headed into the light and I imagined I heard something of great power moving through the forest not too far ahead.

Water

"To the West
Where Father Sun goes
To bring to us darkness,
So we may see the universe
And search for the questions
Of our life."
—L. Kibby

Beauty in Brokenness

 I took a walk today back to the river with the One-Who-Sees. A number of branches were blown off during a recent storm. My initial thoughts were of imperfection glaring in the ragged breaks. Then it occurred to me, haven't there been storms before? Haven't these trees, this forest, experienced breaks in the past? Isn't the uniqueness of each tree and the entire forest the result of the culmination of wounds from those storms?

As I stepped back and took another look it was clearly a unity, a work of art. Even that tree and that one with the top broken off long ago! Every individual, scars and all, crafted uniquely by storms, were now a wonder of beauty through my shift in perspective. Who was I to determine their worth and pass judgment upon an apparent fault?

People are trees. We get blown around, broken and crash into others all the time. As a result of our wounds we are marginalized by the judgment of others as well as our own self-criticism. Today it became clear that what is often considered imperfection can be received and embraced when seen as part of the whole. Creator sees the bigger picture, knows the storms, and holds our brokenness. The One-Who-Sees graciously understands the beauty behind the wounds.

Back by the river a pine leaned against an elm and willow for support. They didn't seem to mind embracing the beauty of their neighbor's brokenness.

Drawing Near

Maker of the Four Directions, help us to consider the east that every morning proclaims rebirth and faithfulness, a new beginning. Let us take it not for granted for in doing so resides the death of our thankfulness and humility.

Green Fire of our Being, help us to consider the south for she speaks of grace as her warm winds bring the breath of life. Let us take it not for granted for in doing so lie the roots of pride and arrogance that strangle our grace toward one another.

Sky Painter of the Day's End, help us to consider the west and its call to rest in order to look within so we can look beyond. Help us to slow down and take it not for granted, for without self-examination, thoughtlessness directs our path.

Endless Understanding, in mercy draw us to consider the north for in that white silence speaks the patient wisdom of the elders. Let us take it not for granted lest we become vain and reckless fools. Wake us gently to higher consciousness. Bring light to sleeping eyes, Loving Father, that we may consider your embrace of the immense incalculable heavens and its reaching down even to our own small hearts. For in such knowledge awe loosens the grip of fear that often haunts us.

Lover of All, Lover of even me, in all the directions, I/we are never alone, never out of your compassionate gaze. This is the eternal song. Your voice sings the harmony of our union. Oh, that this truth could seize more of the world; then in the grasp of this reality, self-judgment and the sentencing of others flies away.

Gravity

 In five cold months I hadn't heard the sound, a faint subtleness mixed within the hum and whirr of bending branches in the wind. It couldn't be far away. I stooped to peer through a thicket and sure enough, there it was—flowing water, the necessity of all life, unlocked and giving itself without reserve to the draw of gravity, a tiny rivulet searching for the lowest common denominator, joyful tears on the cheek of our Mother.

A gathering of twigs momentarily pretending to be Grand Coulee Dam soon gave way and the rivulet became a rush. As I descended the slope another and another joined the parade. Here and there a pond of stillness, but the march could not be contained. What had started with a single drop was now a cascade of freedom as innumerable others joined in gay laughter. Each united with brothers and sisters in an ever-increasing hymn of joy on their seaward journey.

Suddenly, into my mind's eye and the ears of my heart came the teaching that was before me. This Scripture of Creation was speaking, "From every corner of this watershed, I draw all to the sea."

Each drop had experienced a different path. Journeys for some were confused. For others suffering had obscured, darkened, their passage. Some proudly mused they knew the route and foolishly cast judgment on those of agnostic leaning. Our lives are a drop in the current of time. We flow inexorably toward the great eternal sea. We cannot withstand the gravity of time.

In that single moment as the stream moved before me and Creation spoke, a trust floated upward from deep within, a faith that the sea lovingly embraces each drop no matter where its pilgrimage has taken it. This is the destination of all life.

An Audience of One

Picture this: You and I are balanced on one of countless charcoal boulders stretching as far as we can see up and down the middle of an inconsequential, almost dry, river bed. This corridor has the appearance of a canyon as it is bounded on each side by a nearly straight wall of leafy greens—maple, oak, ash, pine-tops of which gracefully bend under the urging of a breeze. This tortured passageway is softened along its flanks by a restricted tangle of grass and mid-August sedges. Our ears are gently bathed with the slosh and burble of water as it bumper-cars its way down this highway to the sea. A wren scolds us while at the same time probing crevices in the bark of a hemlock; and overhead, as its name infers, a fly-catcher darts and swoops at a cloud of insects for lunch.

This is a small section of the Little Eau Pleine River that runs through my property. This is heaven here-and-now, you and I communing, experiencing, relating, hearts beating with the one rhythm of creation. Exchanging breath with the Spirit of the Universe.

Many seek a divine/spiritual reality confined within the walls of an institution with dogmas and doctrines. But, Spirit by nature will not be confined to anyone's paradigm or tradition.

As we stand balanced on these rocks Spirit is singing in this canyon of the Little Eau Pleine. Spirit is always singing, rejoicing, out there and within our beings. It just takes eyes to see, ears to hear, a centered and quieted heart.

Near a tiny pool, between the sedges and boulders four dragonflies, wings of velvet and midnight, bob around each other in gay dance, their slender metallic cobalt blue bodies iridescent in the light. Clearly, they are filled with Spirit's ecstasy expressing the mind of God.

To their right, perched slightly above on the edge of overhanging stone sits a single viewer. Its wings lace like, transparent. Its body, cadmium red, radiates passionate approvable. What a grand performance for this audience of one!

As you and I begin to retreat downstream, boulder to boulder, we too become aware of our audience of One passionately relishing our dance along the Little Eau Pleine.

Faithfulness: Light of the World

Looking across the field a different spirit baths the scene as mid-September slips above the horizon. The light has changed, become softer. It is the Light of the World that urges my relations to ready themselves for winter. Squadrons of swallows skim the ponds. Bear raid hives and squirrel caches, devour berries. A gardener wearing a mask secretly harvests corn at night and the last skins are shed as our armless, legless, friends slither through the duff seeking entrance to south facing hillsides in order for sleep to come gently in the warm earth. As days get shorter and shadows longer, it is the light that directs these lives. It is the light that washes over our sphere, giving, instructing, guiding life in its cadence of perfection.

It is the Light that can direct our lives if we will but stand in it, let it fill our being, renew our mind, expose the love hiding in our shadows. Every human, no exceptions, you, are a creation from birth bathed in the Light.

Yes; ignorance, deception, and erroneous indoctrination may veil—even eclipse—the Light of

Love that is you . . .but ultimately Love rises, Love wins. Let this light throw off the lie of that need for self-protection. Dwell in the Light of the World and it will tow out of you a life that changes the earth. It will drag out your peace, grace and a love that cannot help but give itself away. You shall be as the light of the morning, swallowing the darkness, igniting the eyes of those captured in gloom.

The spirit of mid-September light speaks of rest to come with resurrection to follow. This light speaks of faithfulness. We can trust it, follow it, let it lead. Our relations know this and teach us. They have been guided by it from forever.

Timepiece of Our Night

The beaver pond dried up years ago and was now overgrown with sedges. There, under a three-quarter moon in the dew covered grass I spread out an old canvas and sat down. Leaning back, I let my breathing settle and looked up into the partial face of our celestial neighbor. Without delay I heard her speak:

"I am the timepiece of your night. You and I entangled, traveling in unison, sailing through the heavens. My silver and gold captured, embraced by your white and blue foam. I float upon the tide of the ages. My vision washed with the magnificent greens of forests, radiant hues of your seas, the splendor of gray mountains, rich browns/tans of deserts, and the dazzling reflective poles. Your oceans swimming with life, the firmament above pierced by flight, the stampede and glory of great beasts, the rise and fall of your civilizations.

"I have witnessed the visible red stain of warfare, acid-green of affluence being poured into seas and air, tar-like blackness flowing from bigotry, hatred and the blister yellow religion of greed. I wept over your ignorance and beheld your murder of the innocent One. Yet, I have never turned my back.

"I feel the exhilaration of your potential divinity. I know of your joys and love. Latent in your being, beauty and grace are yours to bestow upon the world. Kindness, gentleness, meekness, goodness already lay within your heart waiting for expression. There are those who perceive; yet there are too many without sight—held captive in the lightless dungeon of a fearful ego. Step back from the abyss, give pause, ponder the good, the true and the beautiful in your hearts. Gain again your intimate presence with the earth. Know that nothing is fulfilled in and of itself. All together in union we have made our voyage through light-years of time. This is the way of the universe, the way of unity and relatedness.

"From where does your pathology of fear, division and disregard surface? Is it not that coursing through your brain is the deception of estrangement? If you knew of your oneness with creation and our Creator the colors of love would restore and reconcile your world. Allow the love that surrounds you, is you, to renew your mind, for in this is the salvation of the world and the continuance of our journey."

Then came silence. There in the dew of that night, in the heart of the universe—perhaps the most gorgeous place in the cosmos, I found myself on bended knee thinking of future generations.

We have the capacity to change. Humanity's predatory relationship toward the gift of creation and each other—can be transformed. We can live in sustainable harmony with brothers and sisters and the world. There is only One World, One Family of Humankind, One Creator of All.

I rose, rolled up the old canvas and stood there musing of wisdom and our interdependent relationship with the universe. As she moved in her great arc across the sky a nocturnal chill condensed my breath into spirit-like form.

Finding Harmony

Before the place where I sit hundreds pass me by, unique, beautiful beings of mystery and amazement. I look out through curved windows seeking a glimpse of each soul as if I were God. Now and then an invisible force will draw one's eyes to gaze into mine and a tiny fragment of understanding is exchanged. A revelation that together we breathe the one breath of creation.

I have taken a moment in this shopping mall to re-center, to regain some mindfulness amidst the folly of consumerism.

"Looking for souls," I call it. It is the quickest way I know to find mine, to bring my scattered being back to its center hushing the dissonance of my song. By this deliberate invisible reaching out for the beauty and essence of another, harmony is restored as love effortlessly rises in my heart like a warm current in a restless sea.

Yes, harmony and love, part of our very nature, shy and polite, waiting to be invited into daily life. There is nothing peculiar or weird, no hocus pocus required to walk in these most supreme attributes of life. Harmony and love arrived with you in the same package at birth. Through our journey, scars and wounds unhealed, misunderstood pain, deception and distraction may shout them into a back corner of our soul and we may wonder if they were only an illusion. But, fact of the matter is, it is through the very ebb and flow of the tides of life, the privilege, if you will, of being hurt, feeling anguish, suffering and our own foolish self-centeredness, that we learn to cherish the mindful state of harmony and love.

I have spent only a few minutes on this bench in the mall. The clamor of all this commotion and busyness is once again set in its place as I have made contact with the core of who I am.

I invite you to give it a try. Sit down, step back, imagine you are the Parent of Creation beholding your children. Judge not. See the beauty and mystery that is every being before you. Love will effortlessly rise, and you will find the song of your soul in harmony.

The Least of These

Wind-chill crept to -65°F driving cold through the cabin walls. Aspirin sized spots of frost appeared on nail heads of the handmade door and crystalline fractals grew on each pane of glass consuming what little humidity remained. Pine popped, snapped in the woodstove adding its voice to the contracting walls, as logs broke free from old chinking.

Finishing off my supper's last morsel of fried perch I heard a faint peep. Soon another and another came from outside my window. I quietly scraped away some frost and squinted into the darkness. There huddled together in a row with tiny beaks parallel to the sill were five Nuthatch squeezed against the glass absorbing what heat they could.

Under the stove I keep a dozen glacial stones to act as a heat sink. Putting on mittens I selected three, set them gently on the shelf under the window and turned down the light. Water soon dripped from the frosted pane pooling near the stones. A sparkle of increasing comfort was clearly reflected from their widening eyes as a waxing moon peeked out from behind the night clouds.

Through that night, while ice split the trees, I tended the fire and exchanged stones every couple of hours for my little friends. They left just before sunrise and the words from long ago came to mind, "Truly I tell you, what you have done for the least of these you have done for me."

Prison of Love

A snap of red darted past me into the bittersweet. I squinted, searching the tangle of vines. There he sat, touching his less adorned mate and offering her a seed. She tilted her head, approved the gift and took it in her beak, a truly cardinal moment in their lives. With a few deft manipulations the husk fell off and down-the-hatch. In a moment he was off again soon returning with a second offering. They moved closer, side to side, clearly in love.

My mind drifted away to past images of doves in a warmhearted relationship—my parents holding hands; dogs, wolves, and fox overjoyed with seeing a companion; cats, tails straight in the air, purring as lithe bodies slide against one another. . . the unspoken language of universal passion.

Love; the interplay of hormones, psyche, need and spirit. Love; the emotion of highest virtue and catalyst wherein the self is dissolved into the "other". Living under this influence, we, like God, cannot help but give ourselves away. Love; the creative impulse of the universe—dispersing, absorbing, rebirthing itself in and around all things as it guides consciousness toward the oneness of creation. In Love's embrace fear vanishes, barriers melt, and abandonment of the self comes naturally.

With the bittersweet in view, I parked myself a short way off, captured by the grip of peace beyond understanding. Peace that overshadows our being when Love's Presence becomes tangible.

The affectionate winged couple took to the air. I closed my eyes, lost and in tune with the fundamental frequency of creation. Ascending with them I entered the "real" and left behind the illusion of disconnection, the deception of isolation.

We are surrounded, imprisoned by Love, always have been, always will be.

Denying River Styx

She bounced across the matted grass, cocked her head to study the earth beneath her and picked a morsel to her liking. Several dozen others were scattered over the terrain. Spring was back. The robins had returned. This grey and faded-tangerine flock swarmed over the field gleaning anything containing energy. Between each snowdrift and rivers of runoff they were filling their craw. The warm south wind bathed my face and I smiled at this wild buffet.

A number of excited feathered ones were following an especially violent stream of cold water. Hopping, squawking, cackling, hurdling one another as they followed the flood downhill in my general direction.

I moved toward to the chaos. There in the middle of the rushing surge was a vole, stubby legs thrashing the icy water trying to keep its tiny pink snorkel in the air.

The riot drew closer and the concerned mob halted, questioning the motives of this human. As he washed by, my heart went out to the little fellow struggling for his life. In only seconds he would be gone, caught in the whirlpool up-water above the culvert draining this field.

When we think of spring we think of resurrection and life. It is the season of new fawns, awakening of insects under the bark, eggs in the nest, and the empty tomb. But, for this wee comrade his journey was nearing its end.

My smile disappeared, replaced by compassion and pity.

Assisted by gravity I sprang downhill over the thawing earth. I grabbed for him and missed as he descended into the churning grave, his small black eyes beseeching the mercy of heaven.

I stood bent over and knew I wouldn't forget this passing moment of such a fragile life. His pleading eyes fixed in my memory.

Then it happened. Up from the whirling maelstrom of River Styx he shot. His tomb could not hold him. I had another chance. He had another chance. Hoping not to miss I spread my hand wide and drove it upon his body.

I had him! My heart and his filled with light.

Dropping him onto a nearby drift he laid on his back gasping, cold and shivering, eyes now closed tight. In a few seconds he stared upward, flipped over and with miniature hands desperately began squeezing icy water from his coat. Upstream, the flock voiced their joy having been witness to his resurrection.

Such is the teaching of life in spring, the season of the greatest miracle.

Prince

 My boot's sole drove hard against the rolled edge of steel. Leveraging the handle, I broke loose the sod, pushing it over, exposing damp humus to the sun. I was disrupting the lives of thousands and they fled desperately from my sight. Forcing the spade again into the dirt I lifted it to the side. A message of terror was being spread in the earth below me, "the end of the world is upon us."

I honor all life and so, hoping, praying for as little death as possible I hesitantly continued my task. Life, the highest expression of an expanding universe. We seek it beyond our blue orb driven by wonder if we are alone in the reaches of space. Alone in eternity. Yet, here beneath my feet was the miracle of multitudes of beings. Amazing creatures like you and I, brought into being by the wondrous work of the Great Mystery. A mystery to which we have ascribed many names, Eternal Mind, Jehovah, God, Brahma, Allah, the Beginning and the End, Gichi Manidoo, Father. Names expressing awe, meant to leave us humble but in love. This mystery in its myriad of forms, expressed in levels of consciousness only the Creator understands, is precious beyond measure. Each form and individual a beautiful revelation flowing from the infinite Divine, conveying a manifestation of the heart of God.

It was here between white pine and oak that I decided to return the body of my friend to the earth, to allow the physical elements of his expression to be reunited with their source. He was a four-legged, given to chasing down ducks and pheasants, riding in the passenger seat and frequently offering curled lips and a snarl to strangers. He had passed on in the night while sleeping by my bed. I helped him go, resting my hands on his side and head, looking into his eyes as the fire left. I wrapped him in his blanket and waited for daybreak.

It took only twenty minutes and a spot in the lap of our Mother had been dug. I lifted him into the grave. Tears and memories uniting with each shovel of earth gently resting on his body.

With the passing of years six friends now lay together in the earth. It is always the same; the mystery of what lies beyond, the inability to grasp life's brevity, hope and love for the preciousness of life in all its forms. These questions, emotions, flow from the aura of my heart and overshadow my mind.

Thanking Creator for the gift and experience of his life, I breath deep to regather my being. I offer tobacco, bow my head and turn toward home. One thing and one thing only do I know as I leave his resting place brokenhearted with spade in hand— humility and love are my close companions.

That Day

The smell of damp humus hung in the air between towering aspen crowding a single-track dirt lane. Stepping without sound into this narrow opening, eyes scanning both directions, I was Azrael, angel of death, here to kill. A muted click told me the safety was off as my finger slid behind the trigger guard.

From eighty yards and slightly downhill, a black image ambled onto the road, lifting nose toward the sky, taking in the coolness and sensing the good life of the day. Slowly, almost imperceptibly, my sweating hands raised the rifle. My cheek lay pulsing behind the sight.

The blast drove wood and steel into my shoulder, shuttered nearby branches, left the sound of death echoing between the hills. Three thousand foot-pounds of energy instantaneously released upon this peaceful, glorious being.

He struggled for cover, collapsing against a limbless dead-fall. Raising his golden muzzle in my direction his eyes met mine asking, "why?" I could not answer, and time stood still. Then with a song I will never forget he turned his face heavenward looking to our Creator and sang out his release from life.

I sat the rifle on dried leaves, leaned forward, palms on my knees, face to the earth, as shame swept over my heart.

It has been over forty years since his story ended. Forty years I have revisited that day. His pelt has been given respect among my sacred things. I have never willfully killed again. The incomprehensible value, wonder and reverence that I see in all our relations became his gift initiated by his death song that day. From that day the magnificent nobility of all beings grows in my consciousness. From that day our spirits were inseparably joined, and my life changed forever. Over the decades he has whispered to me and helped me understand kindness and empathy toward all life. This may seem odd to those who see sport in taking life, but until we meet again, the remorse that gave birth to a higher revelation will forever be my companion.

Between the Bookends of Life

My fingers gently slid along the back of her neck, over a soft shoulder and slipped gradually down her side. A gentle but deep breath told me inner tension was giving way to trust. Her eyes slowly closed as my words of reassurance united our beings. I moved my hand under her back and lifted her feathered body from the snow. Thinking the reflection was her entrance to the sky she had crashed against the glass. What could I do? She and I were helpless, my only offering, sympathy and compassion. I carried her inside and placed her on a towel near the window.

The bookends of life, birth and death, bring profound awe and wonder, confusion and bewilderment. From where do we come—go? To ponder our destiny with honesty leaves us speechless, able to cling only to hope in our ancient stories, our faith.

Miraculously, her eye quivered then opened. She nodded, rested her beak on the towel, moved a trembling wing. What seemed her fate was not to be, as life-giving Spirit returned to animate this fragile life.

To me, the breathe of life, the field of being, seems to transcend this plane of existence. Yet, if the grace that gives me consciousness is only now, it is beauty enough. I remind myself daily of this privilege in order to honor this miracle of the universe.

I set her tenderly back on the snow and stepped to the side. She momentarily studied the scene and then burst into flight resting a short distance away in a dogwood tree. As doves do, she whispered a gentle coo then commenced on her journey into the sky.

Joy and Sadness

It is the end of April. Abnormally hot for this time of year. A flash and a few seconds later the ground shook. Thunder reverberated from across the river signaling the sky meant business. I stepped out from under the porch roof lifting my open mouth to gray sky as it collapsed. A riot of coolness fell onto my tongue bringing my senses alive.

Convection, the mother of this storm, had raised a cloud equal to Everest. Millions of tons of moisture descended, the accumulation of drops beyond number. No two the same. Each condensed around a unique micro center of dust. Trillions of liquid galaxies.

The alleluias of lilies, the praise of bending grass, the ahhhh of young leaves and the sparkling eyes of feathered friends joined the crashing din in worship. Three Golden Eye, migrating north, slid to a landing on the dimpled surface of the river and stretched their necks heavenward. With wild flapping wings they applauded the faithfulness of Creator.

Thankfulness is a peculiar state of being. It rises and falls in inverse proportion to lack or abundance. I have wondered often about the reason, the point of life on this plane of existence, its amazing joys and seemingly profound excess of sadness. It is easy to turn our face toward the sky in thankfulness when cool blessings descend and certainly too much to be expected when darkness, bewilderment, and despair surround. Yet, through decades of musing, I have learned that a cultivation of gratitude can become the underpinning of life, an artesian well from which hope flows.

I stood there in the downpour, a joyous fool lost in that moment of life, filled with a holy carelessness, happy in celebration with all my relations.

Eternal Tides

 A wave, a deep pulse, moved through my body as I wiped the salty brine from my face. Twice daily, the heartbeat of our living earth surges through the oceans. From eternity the tides of the universe and tides of the earth, have spoken the rhythm of Creator's heart. It is the beat of all sustaining love. In all beings, in all that exists, it is the spiritual cadence sounding our oneness.

My rising silver-sky companion tugged the water eastward as I teased the tide's retreat. In the soft chrome moonlight of this April evening I moved among boulders on the shore and happened upon a turtle lodged in a mound of driftwood. Her dark shell dry, legs dangling, head drooped.

I lifted the bleached and twisted pile and she fell motionless on her back. There on the damp sand, as though dead, she drew from my heart empathy many might consider reserved exclusively for our own species. For a momentary glimpse it was as if I looked upon her through the eyes of God and saw the immeasurable value of every being, every aspect of creation, a care and appreciation so deep as to be beyond containment. My mind spiraled outward and I leaned to catch myself upon the driftwood. From this angle I reached down and righted her, giving some dignity to the scene.

A cloud passed overhead, drew me from my trance and called me down the beach. I walked onward to a stream blocking my advance. There I sat upon a bolder, packed, lit my pipe and holding its warm bowl, thankfully considered the privilege of existence.

I stopped again at the ghostly pile on returning up the shore. She was gone. Had she given her body as sacrifice to a night scavenger or had she resurrected and headed out to sea? I like to think she is swimming again. If not here surely within the eternal tides of God.

For Timut, Sabina & Family

eyond three decades have dissolved into history since I first walked the white linen landscape of the Inuit arctic. Eyes pinched shut against the snowy glare, I made my way from gravel beach into town. I was here to pick up a gift, my son, six days old.

From the hearts and bodies of two remarkably sensitive people the little chestnut brown fellow lay waiting. Here, from the cold north, warm love reached southward and in trust bestowed a life to tend and protect.

There is no greater love then to give life, to give life away for another. With their image in my mind every day, I thank them for that trust. I believe they, now from beyond the grave, from their place in the heart of God, would be pleased. Their son, today a man, presents the image of their beings to the world and the world is blessed.

With the silence of the north enfolding our souls I carried the little man back toward the beach as low dark sea clouds stacked themselves in the bay.

Today the green quilted lands of the south are his home but spirit never forgets. Adopted, bonded by blood and trust, our two families remain forever united in one world, one family of man, one Nunaliurti (Creator) of All.

Final Goodbye

I rotated the key and opened the door. Silence, stale air, hovering dust in a shaft of light welcomed me. His home had been closed since that day - four rooms, here along the shore, a simple home now empty, patiently waiting. I stepped into a neat and orderly hermitage filled with odd treasures that had meaning only to him. A marble rolling stick against the wall, a pile of small stones on a shelf, old hats hanging from wooden pegs above the closet, photos everywhere.

He was far from the many but close to the few. He and I had been friends nearly seven decades, each visit ending with a difficult goodbye. Here had lived a being fused and bonded to a small number of persons nearly all of whom had moved away. He knew he was loved but in a peculiar sort of way that made the distance between them the more painful and thus loneliness became his most frequent visitor. Here had lived a spirit with love to give, a warm touch to bestow. A heart that knew those persons had their own lives to live and let itself be broken in the farewells and moving away of friends and family. He had revealed his brokenness to me often.

A groaning sounded from the wood floor as the weight of these memories strode through my mind. I moved through the rooms pondering the speed at which life passes and the precious privilege of relationships. A photo of his wife, family, grandson, the last dog in his life, all sat on his dresser waiting to say, "goodnight." He had passed alone in this bed looking for a hand to hold.

The light outside grew dim and the bittersweet richness of loneliness and love surrounded me. I moved toward the door knowing more deeply the pain of separation, and reaching again for the key, said goodbye one last time.

Tent of Habitation

I found a shrew on the snow today, lifeless and alone, a tiny being who filled only a small portion of my palm, almost weightless, dressed in gray fur. Legs pulled up seemingly to keep warm and eyes peacefully closed as if dreaming, I half expected it to awaken. It did not. Here, in the warmth of my hand lay a body of wonder. Its existence marked by experiences of adventure, fear, discomfort and pleasure, a tent of habitation for the Spirit of Life that only recently departed. Where had this being gone? Looking at the calloused wrinkled skin of my palm the same question materialized about my future.

From the path ahead came a barely perceptible cry, so high and shrill it seemed otherworldly. I caught a flashing glimpse of what must have been friends as they dove down a hole in the snow. I stood motionless, little friend in hand and sure enough they reemerged searching the path. Back and forth, closer, until one caught the smell of their companion at the sight of its passing. Joined by the second, black noses twitching, they seemed confused and again began their shrill cries.

Slowly I tipped forward, reaching, a descending "god" giant returning the one they sought unto the clean snow. They did not flee. Instead, puzzled, silently and gently they nudged their former associate. The question in their minds and hearts the same as mine. Where was the Spirit of Life that only recently coursed within?

We stood immersed in the most primal of questions, shrew and human, the three of us here bewildered and mystified in the face of death. Time passed. Finally, one compatriot turned and meandered down the path. The other, more patient, nose drawing in the last memories of its friend, finally headed off in the opposite direction as if to grieve in solitude.

Once again, I tipped forward, reaching, a descending but now more-humble "god", and respectfully retrieved the body of my fellow being. I stepped from the path, brushed aside the snow and lay this former tent of habitation of the Spirit of Life into the shallow and sparkling grave. In a few months this tiny physical expression of the Great Mystery would be gone, but never lost.

Earth

"To the North
Where the cold winds come from
Bringing to us the seasons
Of fall and winter."

Touch the Earth

Lying on the earth, my back against a weathered rock, I recalled a time in early life when I was frequently occupied with the question, "Who am I?"

As life moved on an illusion began taking root. I became caught up in thinking "I" was what culture, institutions, and authorities in my life told me I was. I was an athlete, a leader in my school. I was religious yet a sinner. I was an obedient citizen, a rugged man. I was defined by the fiction of others. I was a "doing" not a "being". These imposed judgments became the answer to "Who/What am I" and masked the true mystery of my being.

Today, what others think may still affect my emotions, but culture, institutions and authority no longer define or restrict "who I am." The weathered rock against my back tells me I am one with my Mother/Father, the All Parent of Creation. The Ancient of Days speaks to me through this rock telling me that I have been loved from eternity past. This grandfather/mother of the earth whispers, in language understood only in the heart, that I am connected to all things, all people.

Touch the earth. Lay your body down and let the rocks speak. Press your being upon that from which you are given life. Sense the embrace of forever and feel the pulse of the Great Mystery. It is your inheritance, innate within, and waits to be embraced.

Along the Border

 Lying on the earth, my back against a weathered rock, I recalled a time in early life when I was frequently occupied with the question, "Who am I?"

As life moved on an illusion began taking root. I became caught up in thinking "I" was what culture, institutions, and authorities in my life told me I was. I was an athlete, a leader in my school. I was religious yet a sinner. I was an obedient citizen, a rugged man. I was defined by the fiction of others. I was a "doing" not a "being". These imposed judgments became the answer to "Who/What am I" and masked the true mystery of my being.

Today, what others think may still affect my emotions, but culture, institutions and authority no longer define or restrict "who I am." The weathered rock against my back tells me I am one with my Mother/Father, the All Parent of Creation. The Ancient of Days speaks to me through this rock telling me that I have been loved from eternity past. This grandfather/mother of the earth whispers, in language understood only in the heart, that I am connected to all things, all people.

Touch the earth. Lay your body down and let the rocks speak. Press your being upon that from which you are given life. Sense the embrace of forever and feel the pulse of the Great Mystery. It is your inheritance, innate within, and waits to be embraced.

Rider of the Seasons

 Spent the last couple of weeks on the Tex/Mex border listening to coyotes and watching the tarantulas as they head off on predetermined business across the desert. Standing naked in the moonlight, hearing the whispers of Spirit in the evening breeze, I fell into geologic time as I pondered the layers of our Mother Earth exposed on a mesa.

Look! There—a roadrunner with a lizard and a raven seeking easy pickings.

Down along the Rio Grande, Mexican nationals offer me their crafts by leaving them on the stones with a jar for a donation. In the dark they wade back to see if the Gringos were generous. It's illegal, God knows why, to purchase directly from those who live in the sand across the river.

Up in the mountains it's freezing at night and a javelina is complaining outside my pickup. I didn't invite him in. Maybe he is from Mexico and doesn't have a "green card." Kind of hard to get one of those when you don't have a prehensile thumb or a trade.

One day I stumbled across a fellow sitting in a hot spring at the base of a cliff next to the Rio Grande. His clothes hung over a machete and saddle on his small red horse. I could tell he was startled.

"Don't worry, I'm not Border Patrol. I'm not even a US citizen. Relinquished that '83 in protest of America's support of terrorism in Nicaragua."

He seemed to understand.

This brother in the family of man I will not see again until we both cross over the final "border". There, where the deceptions of difference and illusions of the "other" will be evaporated, we will remember our encounter and know our oneness more fully.

You should visit the desert. It unifies the soul.

Build a Nest

From horizon to horizon clouds ran across the sky like steeds carrying knights to war. Below, these charging chevrons of geese were combating a headwind on their way to northern marshes. Everywhere in the heaven were patterns to regard and interpret. I was on my back looking skyward from a bed of matted grass and broken sticks.

Reflecting upon my own mind it occurred to me, every scene that passes our eyes is filtered through the filter of past experiences, training, and indoctrination. Each vision is imbued with interpretation, a slant from what actually lay before us. What would it be like to behold a panorama, an event or a person, without the past forming judgment?

This is the vision of our Creator. Beyond time, with no yesterday or tomorrow, we are viewed within the eternal present in which our All Parent dwells. There is no judgment of the scene that is you or me, only curious joy and embrace of all creation. From our Sun to the Pleiades and Orion, from the molecules in our bones to the most distant edge of the universe, all is ever enveloped in that smile of the Great Mystery.

Upon this bed of grass and sticks I became present, in 11a non-dual state of mindfulness. I seemed to coalesce with all I beheld. From this state of oneness, I was no longer the observer but a participant with the Divine in celebration of reality.

Take your eternal now, build a nest, lie down on our Mother, look to the heavens—feel, smell, hear without interpretation or judgment, know the heart of God.

Adjust your Compass

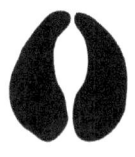Within humankind resides an astounding characteristic. We have called it love. Tagging close behind comes compassion, empathy, kindness, humility, self-sacrifice. The fallout of these tangible attitudes is peace and wise behavior.

Our species, so we tell ourselves, is capable of divine action. I have no argument with this potential, but I have to present an observation: Swimming in our sea of affluence we have lost our love for the earth and thus wise behavior. There is no limit to our consumption and unless we control our selfish appetite, planetary ecocide, that may take only a few decades to unfold, is undeniably the future for our children. Believing otherwise is to live in denial.

Missionaries of materialism baptize the world in the name of over consumption and the tide of extinction is rising.

I admit that much of my life has been hijacked by the false gospel of consumerism. The point of existence is not material acquisition. The point of existence is to grow in understanding the love that fills this planet and encircles us with the benevolence of the universe. The point of existence is to discover and liberate this divine love within your own self for humanity and creation to see. This is what radiated from Jesus and made his life so impacting.

"Consider the lilies of the field—contemplate the birds of the air—it is not possible to serve God, to be alive in Spirit, and yet focused on the material wealth of this world."

The truth of his voice is there for all to experience.

Take stock of your wealth. How much is enough? Are you willing to sacrifice more of the point of your existence for that "which moth and rust destroys?" Resist the dominant paradigm, the diseased idol of Affluenza. "Lay up treasure for yourselves" in love, empathy and kindness. Breathe out thankfulness to our Mother for what she has given and to our Creator for the experience of existence. Only by this will creation be allowed to heal. Only by this will true wealth be known.

Turbo Umbra

I went for a walk with Turbo Umbra today. It's not the first time. We meet often on the trail. Our conversation concerned the nature of the human mind. No kidding. We agreed the phenomena humans call mind is like a jar of muddy water swirling with illusions. Keep the jar agitated and illusions obscure the view. A settled mind, however, my company noted pausing to light a cigarette, is another story.

"A mind that's settled can become disillusioned." Waving away a swarm of flies it continued, "As long as the mind is not at rest, kept distracted, filled with diversions—these illusions obscure reality, but, when the mind is allowed stillness it has a better chance to see clearly and the lies are sorted out."

Our attention was drawn to a strikingly gorgeous reptile in a nearby cluster of leaves. We detoured and headed down hill toward an old orchard.

After several minutes of silence, a muted sigh emerged, and it exhaled a single smoke ring. With this it made a confession. "I'm actually considering a change in careers. Bored. There's no challenge anymore. Most humans are flying autopilot, at the job making an extra buck to pay off their consumer addictions. Every culture on the planet is trading away contemplative traditions for material pursuits. The ability to muse is pretty much lost as the diversions of amusement eat up any remaining time. Distraction is a way of life for your species. I really don't have much to do."

Turning introspective, I had to agree.

We sat in the shade of this ancient grove surrounded by fruit that had fallen in the grass.

"Would you like a bite? Irony intended by the way. Consider this: Through jars of perpetual distraction, you cannot see the reflections of harmony, interdependence, and balance that creation speaks to you, and so you have little of the good, the true, and the beautiful in your lives. Your egos drive you to believe, falsely, that you're always under threat because you cannot see the faithfulness of the One who husbands the universe. So, you competitively push others aside to grasp at illusions thought to bring you security. Your constant distractions evaporate opportunities to get to know your Greatest Friend. So many are so busy for so long that the idea of a mind without distraction is feared. You, therefore, don't have a clue about the glorious and pleasant kingdom that resides within and without. This kingdom could spill over into your world if you took time to let it renew and clarify your mind, let it settle the turbulent distraction in your jar."

At this point we sat there in silence as a breeze came up and nudged more fruit from their branches to within reach on the ground. I stretched, picked up the best looking one and as I did, my advisor squeezed my arm saying, "Don't tell the boss we had this conversation. He prefers you discover these things yourself. Here, try this one instead."

Healing a Thirsty Earth

Our first rain in three weeks had fallen in the night healing a thirsty earth. I stepped out of my tent and inhaled the cool, fresh, clean humidity of washed morning air. Here in a stand of mature maple and oak, the dark, damp crevasses revealed in their bark called me closer. I approached an individual and drew my hands over the texture of its skin. Rough, calloused, with deep furrows, yet made fragile by the rain. Crumbs, like spent coffee grounds, rubbed off on my palms.

Here within these trees life exists patiently; waiting, standing, absorbing their moment in time. Here in these trees was an expression of the nature of Spirit—strength and power, delicate and sensitive, malleable yet indestructible.

I pulled myself closer pressing my cheek against this "being". Its breath mingled with mine and for a moment we seemed to commune in praise and delight. For a moment we knew one another and shared existence.

There are those who judge my activity in these things peculiar, a fantasy, even refer to them as mild insanity. So be it, for there was another insane One who claimed the *"trees sing for joy and clap their hands; the mountains and hills shout,"* and *"even the stones cry out"*.

Let this insanity rule I say. This is what is needed to heal the earth and the mind of humankind. Let Spirit reign and wash away blindness, deafness, lack of sensitivity and the ignorant fear that separates us.

Do not be afraid of looking foolish. Press your hands, cheek and heart against the bark of Spirit and let the healing of a thirsty earth begin.

Theater Planet Earth

At the end of the day our sun kisses the earth's horizon, introducing the night like a father or mother tucking in tired children. From east to west the nocturnal canopy is being drawn across the planet. It is time to review life and ponder the most recent events before they slip into history.

This blanket of shadow and darkness, being pulled up around our chins, calls us into the dreamtime. As it does it also stirs others to arise.

With nose twitching, eyes dilated, searching, the badger exits her cavern. Her grunts, growls and constant internal complaining inform her audience of her mood. Fox, frog and firefly, raccoon, rabbit, skunk and opossum, wolf, deer, mink, flying squirrel, beaver, bear—the total sum of their irritability fails to match up, even though they too work the night shift.

Through the darkness, which matches her mood, like a miniature, organic tank armed to the teeth, she rambles sniffing for "breakfast". Ahhhh, a worm here, a grub there, some roots and grass, maybe a turtle egg or snake for desert.

True to her kind she's ADHD. She pries open a rotting log then dashes to ram her nose into a gopher hole and with three-inch claws sends the earth flying behind her while the local resident exits the back door to safety. Nothing goes uninvestigated as she carries out the performance of her gifts and callings the Great Mystery instilled in her genes.

All our relations, from badger to shrew, bear to raven, fulfill their duties, perform as their script as written. The stage is always alive with drama, comedy, a musical and depending on perspective, tragedy. In heaven and on earth, under earth and in the sea the aria never ceases. It is theater-in-the-round as the curtain of light and night circles our planet.

There are characters with two legs on stage who seem to have forgotten their part, dashing here and there trying desperately to remember their lines, knocking down the set, singing off key, disrupting the harmony, demanding center stage, forgetting they are part of the whole. One has to wonder if they may bring the entire production to a halt.

As rays appear in the east the nocturnal curtain is slowly lifted. Badger yawns and heads back to her cavern. Having played her role to perfection our potential Tony nominee exits stage left.

Eight Tons of Granite

Before me lay eight tons of granite. Eight tons plucked from its home in the Keweenaw, rolled, pushed and carried, rounded and smoothed during its' journey in the embrace of the glacier. Riding on the cheek of this field of ice like a giant teardrop of quartz and feldspar she came to rest in the Northern Highlands an hours' walk east of what is now Hawkins, Wisconsin.

Thousands of her kind, but smaller, were scattered over the land as the blue ice retreated. Slowly, patiently, spruce and moss advanced. Eventually pine, maple, alder and ash nestled around her as primal forest recaptured the scene.

Millennia swept on and the first heat of human fire blackened her flank. More centuries passed, and many hands of the ancient ones touched her side. She continued in her rest as far away in another glacial carved land, sat a young man seeking Truth under a Bohdi tree, another drove his Hellenistic army to the ends of the known world, and a Carpenter's Son was crucified. Three ships left Spain carrying greed and disease. In due time noble voices were silenced and the ax was heard in her forest.

Today, I stand beside her, the signs of her journey presenting themselves on her skin, the black of ancient fires yet visible. My ancestors lived near here in a board and tarpaper shack of two rooms. It has returned to the earth, but this little sister of our Mother remains.

I spread out my arms and lie down upon her, my face and body pressed against hers. She has absorbed the vibrations of history, the changes of the world we walk upon. Lying there I sense her patiently waiting for me to also seek Truth, to understand the serenity of Buddha, the humility of the Carpenter's Son, and to walk the sacred path of beauty and union. I do not want to leave. I have touched the earth and she has touched me. I have felt healing, sensed her patience and hint of wisdom. I have received life for my soul.

Giniw and the Michipicoten

The climb was steep and randomly blocked by alders. Occasionally a boulder, covered in an eruption of spongy, yellow/grey lichen, provided a respite—something to lean against, catch my wind, refill my lungs with the breath of life.

From my canoe I had glassed the face of this cliff for some time before deciding on a route. Finally, reaching the top of the rock debris along its base I stood overlooking the boreal forest below. A carpet of larch, spruce and pine stretched to the horizon. No towns, no roads, no human sign visible. Here and there a birch reached above its cone bearing neighbors and spread its light green canopy to catch the sun. Each step upward brought an expanding view, freedom to my heart, and love for life.

Along with several black flies, I waited a few minutes for what feeble breeze there was to dry the sweat in my shirt, cool me off. Below, a thin ribbon called the Michipicoten River, my highway into this area, curved out of sight around the bluff to my left. Giniw (eagle) glided over its surface seeking carrion, anything that was easy pickings. I turned and looked upward into the ascending cleft of the rock that would lead me to the top. It was here I would put my faith.

Stones now gave way to near vertical solid granite. I reached upward taking hold of a slender root tracing a crack. With its help I placed the toe of my boot on a lip of stone and began my levitation to heaven. Behind me and above came the cry of Giniw (eagle), "Come up higher!" My spirit soared with her and I found a finger hold for another boost, and another, and another.

Pressing my check against the stone I turned to look outward. I was unsecured, without tether, yet the higher I rose the more fear dissolved.

Was I a fool? A misstep and gravity will have its way.

A diagonally fractured cleft gave me confidence and upward I ascended. Soon the remaining face became smooth, polished. I reached as far as I could, feeling, searching for a way to finish the climb. At first there was nothing. Finally, between the tips of my fingers I barely caught hold of another rootlet and gently, inch-by-inch drew it into my palm. Slowly testing I determined it was anchored up and over the edge.

"Come up higher!" she cried again. Then, as if the root itself lifted me into the throne room of God, I found myself in the realm of spirits.

Giniw echoes the heart of Creator, a heart calling us to "Come up higher—into the Love."

Out of the south a refreshing current of wind blew past and was gone. Far below I could see my small craft on the shore of the Michipocoten. The Cleft of the Rock had led me safely upward.

An Ice Age Remnant

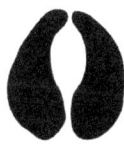 I slowed and turned left on a single-track dirt road. Grass brushed the sides of my truck before towering pines welcomed me to late afternoon shade. Slow, deliberate, like a lazy raccoon, eyes roaming, sniffing my way along the unknown route I shifted into four-wheel drive and began traveling back in time ascending the ancient ridge of an ice age esker. On either side a steep slope strewn with erratic boulders and cobbles kept me pinched in the sinuous route. My mind's eye imagined the primeval landscape, remnant glacial blocks, braided streams and a mammoth family following the retreat of the ice northward.

Returning to the present I noticed the forest beginning to open. Through the trees I caught sight of the lake and was soon parked near cattails along the shore. Wading into the shallows with fly rod in hand, the water's chill took several minutes to get used to. I attached a black gnat to the leader and like an inverted pendulum my arm began the rhythmic pitching, gracefully whisking my tiny bait along the reed edge.

Time stood still as the cadence of my movements shut down all distraction.

There are no barbs on my hooks and fifteen-released-panfish later the sun had moved below the horizon allowing a half moon to enchant the lake's surface. I mused over the passing of time. Having been birthed thousands of years before, this undersized lake was home and refreshment to countless beings as their lives passed and other generations followed. The crickets singing, call of a nighthawk, lapping of water on stone, cracking of the ice each winter—all these timeless sounds enjoyed for centuries by each living thing playing out its journey. It was an honor, this particular day, to sign the lake's guest book registering my short visit into its story.

In the twilight I watched the mists that rose from its surface. Like time they cannot be grasped or held. I had the privilege of a brief moment in the history of this lake. A moment, like every moment, that passes and ascends into memory.

I thanked the spirit of this lake for its kindness and beauty then returned to my truck behind the cattails. In the moon's light I retraced my tracks backward in time along the esker and headed home believing eternity would be as this day.

Our Daily Bread

It was a warm day by northern standards. I stopped in the shade, pulled the pack from my shoulders and let it drop to the ground. My panting friend was glad for the rest and collapsed close by. Taking a deep breath, which evolved into a yawn, I sat down and let my back fall into the burden I had dropped. It was dead calm. Only the rapid breathing and slowly waging tail in old leaves engaged my ears. We merged into the surroundings as if always having been there. Soon our bodies and souls became still and our eyelids heavy.

Half-awake, I became aware of what sounded like the clatter of cellophane wings in our presence and the slight pinch of tiny feet on my hand. With eyes partly open I looked into the inquisitive gaze of a copper bodied dragonfly. She titled her head side to side staring into my face. Her four wings twitched, she looked upward and launching into flight snatched a mosquito from the bill of my cap. With an imperceptible communication she summoned others and soon a half dozen X-wing craft were hovering nearby to join the feast.

I was drenched in sweat but surely it was the smell of my canine friend nearby that kept attracting the mosquitoes into the hunt. A wing clatter preceded each foray as they shared the cuisine. This was no feeding frenzy but a tactical organized communal action meeting the day's need.

I looked over at my furry friend whose tail was still sweeping the leaves and it crossed my mind that unlike the fear driven greed of my own species these relations harvested only what was needed for the moment. There was no fearful drive to hoard or amass. They knew Creator would supply, and so they were present to the only time that exists—the now.

I was drawn from this reflection as tiny feet again landed on the helipad of my hand. We smiled in interspecies communion then with a cock of her head and quick clatter she departed.

I took another deep breath, rose, lifted the pack and we continued our journey, content in body and soul.

Freedom on the Fringe of Our Galaxy

The rhythm of my oars in the humid night air rippled outward as I glided silently, parallel to shore. Leaving the bay my eye caught hold of three distant fires, camps of other souls seeking solitude and the elusive fusion of self with the transcendent. I floated through the night, breathing in the dampness, watching the silhouette of trees against the backdrop of our galaxy. An occasional frog launched itself into the black lake as I invaded its zone of comfort.

Suddenly an explosion of water! To my port side a young family of ducks was startled from their sleep in the reeds. A baker's dozen, distraught and thrashing, madly peeping ducklings surrounded my boat until, regrouping in the safety of open lake, they headed for the island.

Adrenaline ebbed, my heart slowed, and I rowed on. Nearing the outlet several lily pads brushed my bow. I settled in their midst and waited. Earlier that afternoon a pike had given follow to my bait, a big fellow, 12–15 pounds, 40 inches.

Quietly, I snapped on a floating midget spinner and cast it along the weed edge. A listless retrieve with occasional jerk set up a tasty surface noise I knew would draw curiosity for twenty yards underwater.

The night's fingernail moon rose over my stern and I continued working the edge, slowly moving toward the outlet. Just before the lake's surface began sliding downhill, transforming into the Red Cedar River, he hit.

Into the darkness he ran pulling my consciousness with him. I thumbed the spool. Kept a taught line. Played the tension enough to tire this gatekeeper of the river. A lethargic current caught hold of my boat drawing us downstream. He battled, wedged himself to the bottom, tried to run again. My bow struck a rock and lazily spun in midstream. He was wearing out. The distance between spent fighter and my boat was narrowing. I teased him to the surface as his eye caught reflection from the stars above. Considering his strength and beauty, bewilderment and will to live, I reached down with my pliers and slipped the barbless hook from his jaw.

He and I were free and together we gazed upward into a starry universe beyond the comprehension of both our minds. Enveloped in the backdrop of eternity, two individual beings had united themselves through the struggle and wonder of existence. We had lost ourselves in the singularity of the one eternal moment and knew the joy of thankfulness.

He swam upstream and left me alone as I began pulling at the oars. In my mind I can still taste the dampness of that night here on the fringe of our galaxy.

The Earth Speaks

Water covers my boot as I step from the canoe. Of all the stones that lay on the beach two stared upward into my eyes. Freeing one with the blade of my paddle I harvest it from the sand. My fingers trace its shape, sensing the influence of a thousand centuries. In my hand time is condensed, deep and patient beyond comprehension.

Picking up the other, I hold them together in my palm and press the pair to my chest, two tablets of stone imprinted by the finger of God in these Holy Lands. I close my eyes, centering down for what they may have to tell me, listening with my heart for words not heard with the ear or spoken with the tongue. Here, on the shore of the Chippewa, an inner stillness ascends as the earth speaks:

"Creator's hand sustains the life of every creature, the breath of all humankind, sculpts every hill. Ask the animals and they will teach you, let the fish in the waters inform you, the birds of the air sing their knowledge to your spirit. Let your heart hear the Scriptures of Creation. Her communion is love."

A tear of gratitude forms and slips from my eye onto the sand. Yes, the earth speaks. For me, no cathedral, no temple, so imparts serenity and awe as does a simple stone, a single leaf. Granite, quartz, pine and oak, beetle and gazelle, the waves of the sea and breeze on my cheek, all, the myriad voices of God.

Returning the stones to rest with their kin, I have again heard the whisper. The earth speaks, for these are the Holy Lands.

Born of the Earth

I pulled off my cloths and stepped into the spring. Smooth cold clay squeezed between my toes. Lifting a handful above the water where amorphous shapes formed, melted, my fingers worked its smoothness. I spread it over my legs, arms, face. I sank deeper into the wet bed, feet absorbed in the grip of this creature of clay. We had more than shaken hands; our relationship—clay and human—became indistinguishable. I was the clay, the clay, me. This being, my being, fused together in the mind of God from before the beginning.

All beings, called from the womb of the earth to experience existence, still remain attached—cords never cut, spiritual vitality contingent on their relationship with Mother/Father.

Standing motionless near the spring, masked over with the substance, essence, the source of my physical body, insects circled, curious birds darted by and grass swayed. An allegory of aging began to form as this cloak of clay dried. There, in the brittle shell encasing me, I was awakened to the brevity of our days, our connection to earth and Spirit of Life.

I slipped back into the pool and my being, moistened by living waters, again became pliable and vibrant in the life-giving spring.

Touch the Earth, let earth touch you, inhale Spirit's breath, feel the hands and heart of God.

Spirit

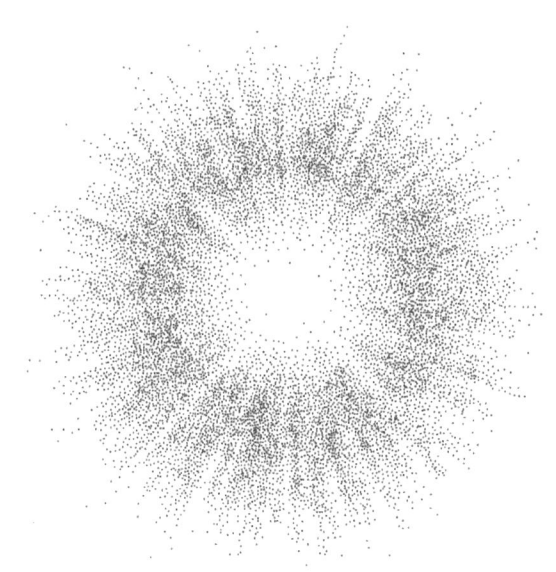

*"Great Spirit Grandfather, Upon the four winds
are my words for strength for they come from the
Heart, Soul and Mind. Words I send to you in a sacred
manner. Great Spirit Grandfather, let all the wisdom,
knowledge and understanding be my strength to
continue on this path that I travel on before you. .
.Now and forever."*
—L. Kibby

The Crucible of Sweet Thankfulness

 Our human experience encompasses the privilege to love or hate; to know joy and terror; ecstasy and grief. We live uncomfortably within this tension of opposites, seeking happiness and elation. It is our nature to flee from the pain and turbulence of life.

In the night garden Jesus too sought to be relieved of suffering. Feeling abandoned, alone when staring death in the eye, he would soon question cynically the meaning of life. While in misery and anguish we too may question or curse the day of our birth as well as our Creator for granting us the opportunity to *be*. We are not liable for our humanity and in this is no shame.

Out of our personal darkness, through the painful labor of life, gratitude and wisdom are being born. It is the seeming contradictions of existence that create the beautiful fruit of humble thankfulness in every unique human soul. It is from this thankfulness that the sweetness of life is tasted.

Try you're best to live believing you are loved within this Great Mystery and when you are unable, remember Christ too had his hour of doubt and uncertainty. Though the embrace and compassion of our Creator is often times indiscernible, it is this paradox of the tension of opposites that remains the reality of existence.

Small Puffs of Praise

Stepping out the door my lungs quickly retreated from the cold. It was still dark. Eighteen below. A vertical shaft of dim royal-purple light hinted at the faithfulness of brave Helios below the horizon. Each boot step on brittle snow, amplified in frozen air, would alert all my relations I was on the move. Deer, rabbits, coyotes, mice would raise their heads and twist ears in my direction. I imagine each one in its own way giving thanks to Creator for their abilities to remain alive in this extreme of winter. Still, my heart formed a prayer for their comfort.

A half hour into the twilight I hear a faint trickle of water under the river ice. I descend the bank, stepping cautiously above the sound below. Here and there is visible the slide of an otter that has been hunting beneath the river's shell. Lethargic crawdads and minnows keep them alive until the frogs and larger fish return in spring.

A few hundred yards upstream where boulders fill a rapidly descending channel, fast moving water creates holes in the ice through which the river's foam ascends. In this intense cold each hole is building up frozen lace castles of froth and tiny ice bubbles. Some are nearly four feet tall, swaying and pulsing as the water pressure changes.

Crawling on all fours up the side of a great turtle shaped rock, I settle down in the snow on its back. From this throne I turn and look downstream directly at the place where faithfulness will again speak. The shaft of royal-purple light is leading us upward to the life-giving sun proclaiming our Creator's warm love and never-ending care.

All though the winters of life may be painfully dark, too long to bear, seem too cold to endure, this Light and Love endures to all generations, in all seasons, for all people.

As brave Helios broke the horizon and streamed a blaze of gold across the river's ice a pine squirrel chattered happily to my left. Small puffs of vapor entering the cold morning air from her praising mouth drew a smile from my face and I sensed the truth of Spirit's presence once again.

Blood on Stone

It was there at the south end of Chilko Lake, thirty miles from the nearest road that I saw the stain—blood on stone, dry but not too old. A life had ended here, an existence sustained only by the tenderness and terror of grace.

My senses heightened, eyes searching the shoreline with its thick tangle of alders. Was I alone? I listened the best I could as waves spilled across the rocky beach. I could see that whatever had died was half carried down the shore and into the bush.

This is the hard and fundamental reality of life, the true nature of things, the supreme law. It is the great give-away. In order for anything to live something must be sacrificed, graciously given away so that life can go on.

Looking closely at the trail of blood it became clear the one taken, the one who had given itself away—mule deer, the one sustained—grizzly. Returning to my boat, I pushed away from shore. I took notice of my rapid pulse. I had come here this second time to enjoy the remote beauty of the Coast Mountains, to be inspired by the perfection of creation. This altar of blood on stone brought me to complete awareness. I was in the present moment, the only real point in time that exists.

At camp that night, as a three-quarter moon glistened on Chilko's surface; I mused over the brevity of existence. Life in all its innumerable forms is the product of grace. Grace—both tender and full of terror. Grace that gives and grace that takes back.

On this plane of existence, you and I have a moment, only a moment. Breathe in this grace with awareness and at each day's end let thankfulness be the last words to pass through your mind and lips - for this is the true nature of things.

A Soft, Quiet Voice

I couldn't see it but there was something in the air, subtle, yet unmistakable. If you were distracted by the other more glaring and harsh realities you might easily miss it.

I was hiking the Ice Age Trail less than a kilometer north of the landfill.

No, it wasn't the conspicuous smell of garbage infused with maggots and rot. It wasn't the exhaust from dozers wrestling the earth to cover sponge-like piles forced from the anus of each giant green truck. That was beyond question the dominant orthodox reality, but every now and then a delicate breath infused with the clearness and sparkle of life would waft through my mind whispering:

"Turn aside. Center down. I speak a higher reality if you will look for me."

I slowed my pace, listened, looked, mindfully inhaled the air. I stood still, centered in that moment and place. Once I did it became evident.

In what appeared to be deliberate—petite effervescent white blossoms were broadly strewn about the forest floor. Now on my knees and bowed before them I drew close with my nose. Yes! These were the dazzling little spirits whose communication with still small voice I had sensed.

Here with head down, humble, listening and sensing the other reality within the prevailing atmosphere, I may have appeared odd, crazy, even possessed, but the truth is. . . these wee beauties spoke of a transcendent divine essence. An essence that, if we will but center down, look humbly and smell the whispers of our hearts, we can all experience and possess. It is the experience of a benevolent universal love being spoken by the still small voice of the Great Mystery. A voice perfumed by the Spirit of God. A smell that charms, attracts and embraces us all.

Consider the Heavens

 It's eleven pm and still eighty degrees. Humidity fills the night sky slightly obscuring my gaze toward the center of our galaxy. To the southeast Pegasus rides above Uranus and Neptune sails through Orion. Just above the western horizon Saturn lusts after Venus as they make an exit stage left down the plane of the ecliptic. Mars and Jupiter will soon be towed into view by Luna, dressed in her silver beauty. Swift Mercury clings to the sun on the other side of our blue orb and Pluto, up there somewhere, voyeur, hidden in the dark, obliquely circles this humble family of planets on the edge of the Milky Way.

All this, just an orbiting spcc in our local cluster, wheels within flaming wheels, incomprehensible in size, space, distance. Beauties hitherto unseen by humankind. Realities we are unable to yet imagine.

Upon what can this be measured? Distance, size, scale, all is relative. Human consciousness spins out of control in the grasping of this. Comprehension appears possible only in defaulting to an emotional perspective.

A slight shifting of gravel draws my attention and I slowly rock my head and eyes downward. In the dark, two mice, unaware of my godlike presence, are making their way up a badger shaped stone. It must be Mickey & Mini. Their almost imperceptibly shrill chatting, just within my range of hearing, I interpret to be comments on the infinitude above us.

Then it happened. They, me, we, mice and man, dust in the universe, floating in the eternity washing around us, sank into the depths of this sea of space and for a moment seemed to know the number of our days. For a moment we glimpsed each other's frail and immeasurable beauty and the grace that allowed it all. For this one eternal moment revelation consumed our consciousness.

The call of an owl brought us back down to earth. From the box seats in our theater Mickey and Mini leaped into the grass and my state of altered perception passed.

Consider the heavens for they consider thee.

Be That as it May

The faintest of outlines remained on the gravel shoreline. Here, several months earlier the spirit of a fox had departed leaving its physical depiction slowly returning to the earth. A meager arrangement of bones covered in moss, a sparse mat of hair and several white teeth persisted in expressing her corporal reality.

What were her life experiences? Was there value in her existence? Where did her essence go? Did her consciousness continue?

The dissolution of flesh, bone, and sinew is the future of all life. You and I, crow, fox, eel and beetle, exist for but a moment in physical representation. It is the turning of the great circle.

Here at day's end, in the twilight, I paused in reflection on the brief sojourn of all flesh. There is no escaping the fragile humility of our beings. Grace alone grants you and I the experience of this gift called life.

I sat down next to her and wondered how I would be remembered and for how long - a mere generation at best. Have people been able to see into my heart, what is really there? What have I presented to world? How might my being have been expressed if pride had been less, intransigence tempered by meekness, if I learned to esteem vulnerability over defensiveness? When all convictions and philosophies turn to dust in the piercing light of mortality we are unable to deny the vanity that dominates much of life. In that moment there is no disagreement with our nearsightedness.

Sitting there amongst these questions a revelation arose from the sand and stones around us—the Voice of Forever:

"Be that as it may, all of My creation is beautiful to Me. Eternity judges you not."

Through eyes moist with thanksgiving I beheld a pair of ants tugging in opposite directions on one of her teeth. It was apparent they too thought highly of all aspects this fellow sojourner.

Of Mice and Men

It is December in the north. A fresh elegant blanket of white sleep wraps the earth. Through woodland stillness the crack of frost can be heard as branches contract in the cold. Here and there rising upward from within the earth elfin like vapors of warm air ascend an invisible stairway to heaven. Out of the south come low angle streams of light throwing soft shadows over this world. Every cautious step I take, every movement bruises the blissful silence.

The quiet of this dreamland is subtly disturbed by an almost imperceptible frequency. I slowly turn my head downward to the left and see a congregation of deer mice giving heed to one charismatic colleague in a state of prophesy. Several members of the audience turn toward me and a religious experience between interspecies commences.

Tiny black eyes stared into mine and they began to speak in tongues as though I descended on a white horse accompanied by legions of angels, sword in hand.

Next came the explosion as their rapturous gaze gave way to what they perceived as reality. Several leapt into the air, landing on the others. Which way to run, clearly the question at hand! Up and over a nearby stump, down behind a log, under a rock, off on a long-distance race home went the others!

I had meant them no harm. My only emotion was one of wonder and delight. I got down on my hands and knees in the dusting of snow to look over their tracks so fragile and delicate, so slight and tenuous, so filled with fear because of misunderstanding. Into my spirit came the voice of Creator:

"Are you not similar? Of mice and men there is little difference. You run and hide from that which you do not or cannot understand; appropriating violence for self-protection when all the while there was nothing to fear.".

I rose up from the ground musing at the inner voice, a smile on my face. Of mice and men there surely is little difference. From nearby came a familiar frequency and I slowly continued my journey.

Chasing Spirit

For four days he stayed watching, vigilantly waiting for a sign, protecting her body until its spirit might return. For four days he had eaten nothing, considering his beloved's silence. She was his life, all his life. They had traveled tens of thousands of miles over two decades together. This was her last journey south. Here in the Upper Mississippi Wildlife Refuge on the western Wisconsin border her strength gave out.

There were previous brushes with death; the sharp crack of guns, near night collisions with tower cables, several battles with fox and mink, reckless, aggressive boats. Once an entanglement with a steel trap had snapped off part of her webbed foot.

This fall's migration had been delightfully beautiful. With others they departed Solon Springs under full moon and for 200 miles followed the silver ribbon below them as the Namekagon and then the Saint Croix flowed into the Mississippi. It was during that first week she began falling behind as the swift southward pointing chevron in the sky fought the predominant west winds. His devotion drew him back from the flock to encourage her until finally together they lost sight of friends and settled on this sand bar near Trempealeau lock number six.

It was here, in my canoe heading north, that I first saw him standing guard as she rested her head and body against a beached log. Respecting their space and last moments together I paddled out into the current and lodged myself upstream on an old snag. It was clear her final hours were upon them. To honor this sacred scene and the passing of life, I offered tobacco to Gichi Manidoo as is the way of this land.

Eventually the sun settled behind Minnesota hills leaving an amber sky as I left the snag and paddled north to find camp. Behind me, retreating in the distance, I heard his call rising, pleading her spirit's return.

For the next four days my canoe glided through floating fall leaves as life meandered toward winter's great sleep. Muskrat houses were ready for the cold. Young eagles, already the size of their parents, practiced fishing techniques and hyperactive flocks of mallards, pintail and teal dabbled and dived, storing up energy for their southward journey.

Upon my return, riding that ceaseless slope toward the Gulf on the back of Old Man River, I neared the holy spot of four days previous. There he was. There her body lay resting against the stranded log. I set my dripping paddle across the gunwales and drifted closer. He lifted his head and called in my direction as if declaring, "She has left and waits for me." With this he ambled down the beach into dark water. Spreading his wings, he ran across the surface and with several "honks" became airborne lovingly chasing her spirit.

In the advancing current of our individual and collective histories it is ultimately only love that calls to us and which we carry with us into the sky.

Angel of Mist

A subtle vapor rose almost imperceptibly down the center of the river. Here, where the current carried the coldest water, the river's slow steady breath began yielding its spirit to the air above. Like a serpent summoned from deep sleep it began to emerge upstream and down, rising, settling, oscillating with the smallest breeze, a phantom materializing in another dimension.

I sat sheltered under a hemlock patiently watching this being of mist ascend while light rain dampened the forest around me. Each random drop from heaven was awakening the soul and life force of the river. As evening began yielding to night the realm before me became saturated by the silent humid air.

Twenty minutes past and my mind settled into unity with the mystical creature before me. She continued to grow, absorbing, entwining the river and forest. With her frail and delicate nature, she wrapped herself around me, filled my lungs, evoked a sense of transcendence within my heart.

This angel of mist, my mind's escort, reminded me once again of the universal embrace of Spirit, the Oneness I am with Creator, which you are with me. This embrace of love, this irresistible unity is the Ground of Being and knows no distance, no separation. It fills the universe as the spirit of this river, now without reserve, filled the forest.

From a distant place, I could hear the thunderous voice of an approaching storm. I rose to my feet in full consciousness now seeing, hearing, breathing without distraction. Through the twilight and mist I stepped over wet leaves and made my way home, alive with the privilege of having glimpsed beyond the veil.

Qimmik and His Barrel

A rusty barrel sat stubbornly near the remains of an old boat. Sniffing, approving a spot to his liking and lifting his leg, a gray antique of a dog encouraged the corrosion of this squat and stoic cylinder.

As I sat on a crate waiting for the plane out of Grise Fiord I pondered how this old fellow survived the winters here in the high arctic. Despite his bedraggled appearance he appeared to have a layer of fat. I had been stranded here for several days by a late season snow and during that time he had cautiously warmed to my friendship. Now and then I saw him being chased from the town site, no strays allowed, and he had taken up residence in this old upturned boat on the beach with speechless barrel as companion.

I called him Qimmik, the Inuit word for dog.

Figuring I'd never see him again I burrowed into my duffle feeling for my cookie stash. He caught wind, stuck his nose in the air and ambled my way.

Remaining out of reach he stood there, eyes shifting between mine and the cookie.

I tossed the first half. It fell to the ground, was smelled and approved. He snapped the second half out of the air. Reaching for another I asked, "What's your story Qimmik? Why are you all alone?" He answered with a string of drool as my mind wandered to the multitudes of people living on the outside, on the lonely edge of existence.

Many of us, like Qimmik, have been the outsider, maybe even an outcast at times. But, there are those who, unable, or defined as unacceptable in our minds and culture, are permanently consigned to existence with Qimmik under the boat.

Paraphrased words of a long ago itinerant teacher from Galilee came into my head, "I have come to bring good news to the outcast."

Cynically, I mused to myself, "For the outcast dwelling in a cardboard box, where's the "good news?"

With that question floating in mind, Qimmik's tail began to wag. Soon his whole decrepit carcass was shaking, and his cookie-dusted lips turned up in a smile. Clearly this outcast sensed he was being seen for his intrinsic value and accepted for the unique creature he was. At that moment Qimmik was not alone in the world and he knew it.

It dawned on me, this is the good news, and my heart soared in the grip of knowing that I, you, not one creature is alone. We are accepted for who we are and never outcast. We are surrounded by the radiant embrace of our Ever Loving Creator.

The drone of a plane reached my ear as he caught the last cookie and I was soon heading south. I never saw Qimmik again, but on that day nearly four decades ago he was the catalyst for a revelation that has become the ground of my being. All creatures, all people, are seen, accepted and loved, no strings attached, by the Author of Life. I must do no less.

Giigoozens, Lover and Beloved

I shoved my paddle into the stone and headed out from shore. A swell lifted my canoe and I slid down its backside. Last night's storm had left this inland sea still rolling. Gichigami, the Great One, clear, cold, fierce, intensely beautiful.

Gliding past sandstone cliffs, I hear the deep drum of surf within their caves, the call of gulls and tern overhead. My spirit is drawn to this water like no other. I have come here to break apart the crust of my heart. For too long my sight has been scaled over, for too long my ears deaf to the love song that gives me power. Without my All Parent's voice washing the dust from my soul I am but a hollow shell, a dry stick feigning life.

From my meek vessel a prayer rises. When will You draw me from the dark abyss to float high above the deep? Why have You turned Your back? Where is Your voice that lifts me?

Stroke upon stroke I slip away from shore toward the horizon. The rhythm of paddle pushing water is all that is heard. Onward, outward, unconscious of time, my being is taken until, looking behind, only a thin line on the horizon marks my point of departure. Sky and sea merge becoming one and I feel I am alone in the universe, desperately alone.

Arms aching, I coast into stillness, the arch of heaven above, slow gentle pulse of Gichigami below. My hand slips into the chill and as I look down, there near the surface looking back is little giigoozens (minnow). Together we drift, two lives in a vast silence. My little companion moves, nudges my finger and I am lifted by a spark of light in the center of my being.

Slowly from my paddle, drops form circles on the water and my soul drinks of the divine presence. The shadow of a cloud moves over my craft and I turn looking for the distant shore. My tiny finned spirit messenger slowly withdraws into the lake.

Filling my lungs with the breath of Creator I have once again been visited with life and peace.

Elegant Magnificence

It lay pointing northeast, twenty-one paces from base to tip, perfectly straight. There was a day when this stalwart soared above its kin. It had resisted gales for over a century, gave way just enough through tempests in order to endure and carry on its calling. Still, time has a way of bringing humility to all things.

I returned to the center of this fallen giant and leaned into its mass, running both palms over the slivered and frayed surface. Ice and storms had battered this stranded monarch against the beach until not a branch remained.

Emerging before my eyes from the weathered gray timber a vision appeared playing the faces of friends gone before—some by their own hands, some at the hands of others, some by illness, accident and age. My mind became lost within these apparitions, our eyes and hearts fused together in a communion of memories. I smiled, bent my knee to the stones and wrapping my arms hard around this old tree of life I imagined the return of their embrace. I want to think they too, from the dwelling place of spirits, were aware of my thoughts and that I missed them.

I don't believe death is the end, the annihilation of self. I don't understand or possess proof. There's just something inside that speaks transcendence, the presence of an elegant magnificence connected eternally with Ultimate Reality—God if you will.

Decades from now this battered tree will have fragmented into the molecules that made it. But, the reality, the form, the uniqueness and essence that was given momentary expression on this plane of existence will continue forever. Out of the mind of Creator we have come and are never forgotten.

Faith

A barely audible whisper came from my lips admitting my destiny was in doubt. Two hours earlier I had departed the trail and began a slow deliberate walk toward the north in hope of reaching the lake. During that time fine mist began to descend through air at 34° calling up fog from the cold ground and setting the boundary of my vision to a few yards.

Pausing in wooded terrain without shadows I listened to get my bearings. Every direction spoke only in the whispers from the drips of ice melting on leafless branches. In mild revelatory panic, I stood quite literally in an allegory of life. I had no idea where I was or what lay ahead. I shivered, and a chill passed as well through my soul. The recognition that I know little to nothing about life or its direction engulfed me in humility.

Beliefs give me comfort. I am lured, as are we all, to imagine what is beyond and therein rests the wellspring of hope to carry on. Human existence is based on faith, the presupposition that life holds personal meaning and has a destination. Faith, without it the eyes dim, shoulders droop and our steps grow somber. Faith, the essential ingredient for survival in the face of confusion and pain.

Behind a cluster of dense brush, a yearling whitetail materialized and just as secretly retreated into the forest. She brought me comfort in her confidence and trust, an inner sense of companionship in my journey. Lacking a better option, I followed her into the unknown. The fog remained and as the sky began to darken I thought I could hear the movement of waves upon a pebbled shore.

Face of the Deep

Leaves of red and gold fell onto the pool disturbing its black surface. I stepped over a windfall and gazed downward into the water. Surprised and perplexed, I was taken aback at who returned my stare. Out of my own eyes this twin, this interior being, wondered at the person before it. Who was beholding whom?

Confused about the location of my "self" I reached down in search of the real. Probing into the deep, wetness slid up my finger, bathed my hand, and my self-centeredness softened. With this the cage of confinement called "I" opened momentarily and as I stepped outside an awareness of the piercing, fierce and tender, healing eyes of God fixed upon me.

Here in nature, my nature was looking back and in the face of that deep I caught a glimpse of the divine nature of all things.

Suddenly a breeze disturbed the surface and drew my attention. Leaves floated downward through the chill, and reflecting in the eye of my mind was the reality that no one, no thing, is ever beyond the curious and sympathetic gaze of our Father/Mother. My heart smiled contentedly at this while the pool's black surface slowly covered with leaves of red and gold.

One Question Only

Sitting on the edge of tomorrow, our life-giving orb readied itself to dip behind the western horizon. Here in the cool of the day when pastels shade soft edges of clouds and my shadow grows long, in the hour when God walks in the Garden, it is here that their faces return. They speak to me from my shadow, voices, images visiting from the past, companions who briefly shared their glow and pain during this journey.

The face of a schoolmate who took his life after Vietnam; the passing last sigh of my dog as he lay near my bed; beings whose lives I ended, whose lives I have abused or simply ignored, along with those lives I blessed; the look in my grandma's eyes knowing it was the last good-bye; my mom, while I held her and spoke of love as she left this world; the pensive smile of my dad reconsidering his fatherhood; the beauty of my son and the tears welling up my daughter's eyes as our visits end and we travel apart.

One deep resonating theme flows through all these images, one question only rises from the shadow I have cast. "Have I loved?"—This alone is the singular issue of the soul, the transcending question that slowly rises out of the shadow of existence.

Our shadow speaks. Embrace its voice, its probing questions of kindness, compassion, and friendship. Our life-giving orb, our celestial timepiece, pulls us toward the western door and the eternal tomorrow. With each passing day the shadows fused to our heels grow longer, following us to the horizon and beyond.

Final Word

From beetle to bear, hawk to anole, all our relations appear to live out their lives in the spirit of their kind without question or little deviation. The privilege of existence given to humanity, however, is one of discovery. Who are we? Who am I? What is our role? On what path am I to walk? What does it mean to be human? What, after all, is the point of existence?

The map of every life is a journey intended to bring us home. It is a pilgrimage of consciousness in which the experiences of life tug us outward and upward. From the selfish realms of the egocentric and narrow ethnocentric mind, to the liberty of world consciousness and cosmic awakening, you and I are being drawn to the enveloping Divine Love.

Our journey cannot be forced. Instead, it is a yielding to Spirit's all-pervading presence and in this yielding, the surrendering of the will and the emptying of our fearful selves, we grow in mindfulness of our union with Ultimate Reality. Our destination is not in some far-off land, some distant place. Instead it lies ever present within the nearness of our heart.

The stories you have heard are intended to open the heart to timeless Love and the peace that passes understanding. To behold the face of this Love, to kneel within the rapturous embrace of the universe, is the ever-present privilege and destiny of our journey.

In some small way I hope these stories have touched your spirit, brought you a sense of the divine, led you closer to a life of holy-carelessness, and enlivened the child that is you.

***

"We shall not cease from exploration, and the end of all our exploring will be to arrive where we started and know the place for the first time." T. S. Elliot

'Til We Meet Again

When the Earth's last picture is painted
And the tubes are twisted and dried
When the oldest colors have faded
And the youngest critic has died
We shall rest, and faith, we shall need it
Lie down for an aeon or two
'Til the Master of all good workmen
Shall put us to work anew

About the Author

James (Pep) Washburn (b. 1949) born in Wisconsin, has travel extensively through the wild regions of North America. His explorations have taken him from Mexico and the Bahamas to the Coast Mountains of British Columbia and Canada's Ellesmere Island, 500 miles from the North Pole. Whether by canoe, hiking, single engine plane, snowshoes or pickup truck, North America's wild places and indigenous people are the essential ingredient of life underpinning an inclusive worldview.

He spent thirty-three years in public education and was nominated for Wisconsin Teacher of the Year in 1983. His first book, *Touching Spirit: The Letters of Minominike,* has been published internationally by Zahrada Publishing of Turkey and Kal-ba Publishing of USA.

Touching Spirit:
The Letters of Minominike

More from Kal-Ba

Written in the pristine environment of the northern boreal forest, Tulugaq Kagagi muses over a series of letters, wthe vernacular of his grandfather, he recalls his life experiences and the spiritual teachings these events have brought him: transforming his life and worldview.

Through the writing of one man and the inner thoughts of another, we too live through wrenching pain and revitalizing joy and peace. From death to life giving ecstasy, we follow the life journeys of two men separated by generations and culture as they find meaning and rest for their lives.

With the drowning of his parents in 1928, a white infant is orphaned in the Canadian north. Tulugaq Kagagi is lovingly accepted into the home of a childless Ojibwa/Inuit couple, Peepeelee and James. He leaves their home in his teens to continue schooling at seminary in the south.

The next thirty years of his life is spent in traditional religious vocation. During this time the enfolding of Spirit, its peace and presence slowly fade from his life. In midlife, upon his adoptive father's death, he returns to the cabin of his childhood and discovers a series of letters written by his great-grandfather, Minominike. His religious education and worldview is challenged by the unconditional love and truth expressed in these letters. As he reads the words of this old man's life his heart is returned to a time of embrace and spiritual oneness that he has not known in decades. Feeling the wind of the Spirit and sensing the inner whisper of a still small voice, meaning and love are again awakened in his heart.

We travel with him on a path of revelation opening his heart to the unity and benevolence surrounding us all. This is a novel that pierces the core of humanity's longing for inner peace and opens for us the simple joy of being. The letters of Minominike bring insight and encouragement to live in the reality of transcendent love.